Contemplation
and Community

Contemplation and Community

A Gathering of Fresh Voices
for a Living Tradition

Edited by JESSICA M. SMITH
and STUART HIGGINBOTHAM

Foreword by TILDEN EDWARDS

Afterword by MARGARET BENEFIEL

A Crossroad Book
The Crossroad Publishing Company
New York

The Crossroad Publishing Company www.crossroadpublishing.com
© 2019 by Jessica M. Smith and Stuart Higginbotham

Copyright in each chapter in this collection is reserved by its author, each of whom has graciously granted permission for its use in this collection.

Crossroad, Herder & Herder, and the crossed C logo/colophon are registered trademarks of The Crossroad Publishing Company.

In continuation of our 200-year tradition of independent publishing, The Crossroad Publishing Company proudly offers a variety of books with strong, original voices and diverse perspectives. The viewpoints expressed in our books are not necessarily those of The Crossroad Publishing Company, any of its imprints or of its employees, executives, owners. Although the author and publisher have made every effort to ensure that the information in this book was correct at press time, the author and publisher do not assume and hereby disclaim any liability to any party for any loss, damage, or disruption caused by errors or omissions, whether such errors or omissions result from negligence, accident, or any other cause. No claims are made or responsibility assumed for any health or other benefits. Printed in Canada.

Book design by Tim Holtz

Library of Congress Cataloging-in-Publication Data available from the Library of Congress.

ISBN 978-0-8245-5051-6

Books published by The Crossroad Publishing Company may be purchased at special quantity discount rates for classes and institutional use. For information, please email sales@crossroadpublishing.com.

MIX
Paper from
responsible sources
FSC® C004071

From Jessie:
To the Shalem community,
and to all the ordinary mystics,
holy and lovely beings of God.

From Stuart:
To Lisa and Evelyn,
my harbor and my heart

Contents

Embodiment, Compassion, and Healing

In Memoriam

In the process of writing and editing this volume, Fr. Thomas Keating passed away. Not long after we gathered in Snowmass, Fr. Thomas moved back to St. Joseph's Monastery in Spencer, Massachusetts, to receive more focused medical care. As the weeks went by with writing and compiling, those of us from Snowmass remained in touch with each other and the wider network of those drawn to the contemplative path. They were thin days indeed, and they gave our work an added poignancy.

The intensity grew when Fr. Joseph Boyle, the beloved abbot of St. Benedict's Monastery who had welcomed us with open arms, was diagnosed with terminal cancer. He and Fr. Thomas died within days of each other.

Who would have known the past two years would be such a liminal time and space? But, having said that, aren't all times such?

As we look back at our time at St. Benedict's Monastery, we can still see that time of shared silence on the last day. As we sat in the circle and looked out at the valley and mountains beyond, there was Fr. Joseph and Fr. Thomas, sitting alongside us, holding the Light they had held for so long— and challenging us to hold the Light as well. With the eyes of our heart, we could see that the circle we shared extended far beyond the confines of that beautiful space and time.

One day, when a few of us were visiting with Fr. Thomas, someone asked him why he had thought to bring us all there.

Why call this gathering? He smiled, looked at us, and said simply, "I just thought it would be a good thing for you all to meet one another." It was a good idea, and we all promise to do our best to remember what you all have taught us.

Introduction

TILDEN EDWARDS

The four of us were eight thousand feet above sea level, seated together in a meeting room of St. Benedict's Monastery near Snowmass, Colorado. Out the window we could see snow-capped mountains above the beautiful valley of the monastery. It was a fitting location to reflect on the turmoil and the hope of the world beyond and in us.

We shared something in common. Each of us was the founder of a spiritual center of hope, grounded in a fresh awakening of Christian contemplative understanding and practice. One of us, Fr. Thomas Keating, a member of the St. Benedict's Cistercian community, had invited us to meet for these three October days in 2016. He had been the abbot of his Cistercian community in Spencer, Massachusetts, for over twenty years before coming to St. Benedict's. About forty years ago, he along with two other Cistercians—Basil Pennington and William Meninger—began a contemplative movement called Contemplative Outreach, which brought to life a form of twice-daily Christian contemplative prayer called Centering Prayer. Centering Prayer groups now exist in at least forty countries. Over the years, Fr. Thomas has authored many valuable books and videos on contemplative prayer and traveled far and wide for in-person teachings about it. Now in his nineties, he felt a call to bring together the four of us to pray and dialogue about how our organizations could collaborate more fully in bringing contemplative awareness, and its personal and societal fruits, to more people in the church and world.

One of the four people he invited was Richard Rohr, a Franciscan friar who has become one of the world's most articulate advocates of contemplatively grounded practice, understanding, and action. In the process, he has presented an "alternative orthodoxy" found in St. Francis and throughout the long lineage of great Christian mystics and theologians. It has received a tremendous ecumenical response from people around the world. Fr. Richard founded his center, the Center for Action and Contemplation, about the same time as Fr. Thomas. His many bold and insightful books and videos offer what a mature contemplative grounding and its fruits in social action can mean for the church and world's well-being and spiritual deepening. His online and residential teaching programs draw a great many people. Fr. Richard's challenging "daily meditations" now are received by as many as three hundred thousand people around the world.

Fr. Laurence Freeman was the third person invited. He is an English Benedictine who was the protégé and successor to Fr. John Main's movement for the twice-daily practice of a mantric form of contemplative prayer, simply called Christian Meditation, grounded especially in the early Christian Desert Mothers and Fathers experience and understanding. The World Community for Christian Meditation, his international organization begun in 1975, now has meditation groups meeting in over ninety countries. Fr. Laurence's insightful writings and talks around the world are extensive, including outreach to teachers, children, and the incarcerated, and to workers in the health, business, and other societal sectors, as well as to churches and religious communities. He also has developed a special program for

Benedictine oblates that includes a commitment to the twice-a-day practice of John Main's form of Christian meditation.

I am the fourth person. After some years of working as a priest in an inner-city Episcopal parish in DC and then heading up several ecumenical centers focused primarily on societal concerns during the civil rights and Vietnam War period of the 1960s, I helped to begin the Shalem Institute for Spiritual Formation in 1973. I was its executive director for twenty-seven years. Although I'm retired from its leadership, I still offer some Shalem seminars. I also continue to write contemplatively oriented books and articles and teach an annual e-course on "living from the spiritual heart." Shalem's ministry offers, among other things, extension programs grounded in contemplative awareness and practices for the development of spiritual directors, leaders of retreats and contemplative prayer groups, local church clergy, young adults, and organizational leaders of different kinds of institutions. It also helps people who primarily seek personal spiritual deepening. Shalem Korea is an expanding independent ecumenical center helped into being through Shalem's work with contemplatively oriented Korean Christians over the years.

All four of us knew one another from past encounters so we weren't strangers around that October meeting table. We spent some time talking about what our organizations were doing and caring about recently. We all shared an underlying passion for fostering contemplative awareness as the intimate heart of Christian understanding and practice and their overflow into called-for compassionate church and societal envisioning and action.

That awareness can be spoken of in many ways. I sometimes speak of its beginning in terms of the hunger for Home, the restless yearning in the human soul to realize a deeper identity than the egoic self offers us. That little sense of self is dominated by a sense of separateness. That separateness leads us to a sense of fragility, fear of loss, and an exaggerated need for protective power and control. We're left enthralled by a small sense of self that is never finally satisfied, and rightfully so, because we are made for more than that.

We might catch glimpses of the "more" in moments when our egoic self is temporarily in abeyance—as when we're caught up in a beautiful sunset, or a child's innocent freedom, or a spontaneous sense of compassion—but these glimpses are just that, and we easily regress to egoic self-centeredness. We may take up psychological counseling or other means to help cope with our ego-neediness, and they may indeed help us bear our lives and situations more acceptingly and rationally, but we're still putting the center in the wrong place. Early in the book of Genesis we read that human beings are made in the divine image. That identity recognizes a deeper, fuller self than our ego image offers us. In the long lineage of contemplative Christian tradition, our true center is found elsewhere.

The early Desert Mothers and Fathers are assuming that "elsewhere" when they advocate letting our mind sink to our heart. The spiritual heart is a different faculty of presence and awareness than the ego, and it's different from the thinking mind. Contemplative practices aim to draw us to that truer place of our identity, leaving us more vulnerable to the Spirit's yearning for us to find our true Home in the spiritual heart. The Spirit that Jesus invites us to receive most deeply lives there.

In the heart center we find our truest identity inside of God, and God inside of us. We are not ultimately separate from God. This is the mutually loving intimacy with Abba that Jesus knew. In times of such graced realization we can be given a sense of authentic freedom, confident trust, inclusive belonging, authentic vocation, selfless compassion and joy. From that heart center God's Spirit in Christ helps us let go of what we hold on to that is in the way of our wholeness in God and aids us in fulfilling our part in the ongoing creation of the peaceable "kin-dom." In such heart-centeredness we can find, then, that our functional egoic self, as well as our conceptual minds, feelings, imagination, and bodily senses, can become integral collaborators with the heart's awareness and callings, rather than competing centers of identity and agency.

Frs. Thomas, Richard, and Laurence would word this contemplative theology in their own ways, but whatever words I've heard or read from them I believe would lead to their nodding their heads to the gist of what I've said, as I have nodded my head so often to what they have said over the years. There's no one right way to word contemplative awareness. The immediate reality of contemplative awareness is more than any words can adequately convey. It is a nondual awareness, a "not one, not two" awareness of our paradoxical union with the deepest reality that we name God.

That deep identity frees us from ultimately defining ourselves in terms of any cultural, ethnic, racial, gender, sexual orientation, political, class, economic status, egoic individualism, or too-narrow religious context. This is part of what makes contemplative awareness so crucial in our divisive world today. We see those narrower identities moving beyond their functional place in human life and becoming *ultimate* identities. The result includes multiplying conflicts among individuals and groups, and often in the end a sense of that lesser identity failing us as it proves too narrow and destructive of inclusive human belonging in the gracious One. When any of these narrow identities become our *ultimate* sense of identity, we find ourselves worshipping an idol, and idols never save us, never show us our true wholeness in the divine image.

There is a desperate global need to discover and embrace our deeper, wider identity that shows itself in our spiritual heart, an identity that engenders individual and communal transcendence of too-narrow identities and leaves us with a sense of compassionate belonging across all human and ecological boundaries. Unless we can find and embrace that place of deep mutual belonging and its forward evolutionary "kin-dom of God" movement that is ever on offer from God, we will be left with a sadly broken and self-deceptive world. This awareness of the world's situation and the promise of contemplative practice and understanding I think was a background motivating factor in all four of us at St. Benedict's that October.

As the days of our meeting went on, something began to emerge that gave us one concrete way we could go forward together in the year ahead. It was a way of cultivating "young contemplative Christian thought and practice leaders," people we knew who represented the rising generation of leadership that would be among those succeeding us. These would be people in their thirties and forties who could stimulate and support one another in their contemplative understanding and practices, and in their ways of bringing these to people in different sectors of human living.

We decided to focus on *Christian* grounded leaders, even though I think all four of us felt that contemplative awareness in some form is found at the mature heart of all major religious traditions. However, we were aware that there have been many opportunities for interfaith contemplative gatherings (some of which we ourselves have helped to create over the years) but very few where the particular Christian contemplative lineage and its contributions could be the central focus. As Louis Komjathy has written in his monumental *Introducing Contemplative Studies*, interfaith contemplative gatherings often have been tilted toward Asian contemplative traditions, sometimes with an underlying prejudice against Christianity, where its long contemplative tradition has not been known or respected. It hasn't been adequately known among Christians either. But beginning in the second half of the twentieth century, a broader awareness of contemplative tradition showed itself and a growing openness to its significance and promise for deepening individual, church, and societal life. As the last chapter in this book exemplifies, the reawakening of Christian contemplative tradition has often been accompanied by an appreciation of contemplative traditions and practices beyond the Christian, with a sense of mutual enrichment and the Spirit's call to collaboration in creating a more peaceful, just, and spiritually visionary world grounded in contemplative awareness.

We agreed that each of us would invite five young contemplative leaders we knew who we sensed held special promise to further the growing wave of contemplatively infused life in the world, people who could both contribute to such a gathering and who could have their own consciousness expanded in sharing with their peers.

We left one another sensing that the Spirit was in this discernment. Each of us sent five invitations to a four-day "New Contemplative Leaders Exchange" at St. Benedict's Monastery in August 2017. I was amazed to find that every one of our invitees enthusiastically accepted the invitation. An additional invitee, representing the Fund for the Meditation Process also accepted. (That fund was very helpful in providing financial aid needed for the gathering.) When they came together in August, every single one of the invitees showed up. In all my many years of leading conferences and retreats, I have never seen one where no one had dropped out, especially one where the commitment was made six months in advance, and where eight of the invitees were coming from places in Europe, Latin America, and Australia.

The design for our time together was developed with the intention of maintaining a mind-in-heart presence throughout, with various periods of silence, prayer, and questions that evoked a discerning mind-in-heart response. We also had the intention of letting the young contemplatives be center stage rather than we four sponsors; we wanted to remain in the background. With the consent of the other founders, I asked Margaret Benefiel, executive director of Shalem, to facilitate the process of the event, given her long experience in facilitating contemplatively grounded meetings.

From the beginning it was clear that the participants wanted whatever happened together to emerge organically from their shared openness to the Spirit's presence, and they wanted to develop personal friendships with one another. They bonded together so well that in the morning of the last full day, when the founders had been meeting in their own small group and returned for a scheduled plenary meeting, we found a note from the participants that they had decided to take a hike together on a nearby mountain trail, during which they would continue their dialogue with one another along the way.

A continuing frontier for many was how to translate contemplative understanding and practice in such a way that it could be embraced by different ages, ethnic and social groups, and nonreligiously connected yet spiritually open people, and in different institutional settings, and doing so without losing the deep transformational intent of authentic contemplation.

One participant provided a helpful image for bringing contemplation into the church: "Not as the icing on the cake" but as the "leaven in the lump of the whole church's life."

During our days together, some participants expressed the hope that any future gatherings would include poor and marginalized people. A number of participants had serious involvements with such people in their own work, including one who for many years regularly went out late at night in New York City in search of homeless youth enticed by pimps, high on alcohol or drugs, or otherwise lost on the streets, to help them find a way out of a predatory and self-destructive world. Several others taught contemplative practices primarily to poor and marginalized people.

I heard a cosmic as well as personally intimate view of Christ and the Holy Trinity expressed by participants, grounded in such modern theologians as Raimon Panikkar, Teilhard de Chardin, Cynthia Bourgeault, Ilia Delio, and Thomas Merton, as well as in the writings of the founders. I think it was Fr. Thomas who spoke of our group as a manifestation of the Body of Christ in a needed new form, that goes beyond individual friendships and past boundaries yet still highly values formation in a particular contemplative tradition. Several participants saw the Body of Christ, at its truest and most inclusive, as the mind-in-heart *human* community as it's meant to be.

At the end of our four days there was no pressure to plan any future gathering, even though the group was open to whatever might organically evolve in the future (see "Contemplative Practices," by Thomas Bushlack, for a sense of their informal commitments to one another). Thomas Bushlack volunteered to set up an internet site where the conversation and mutual support could continue.

It turned out that there were many people who would have liked to come to that gathering once they heard about it. One participant, Stuart Higginbotham, found so much interest from his bishop and among the clergy and laity in the Episcopal Diocese of Atlanta, as well as people in other denominations, that he helped put together a special southeastern United States contemplative gathering in May 2018 at St. Mary's Retreat and Conference Center in Sewanee, Tennessee.

Before the August gathering, we had asked participants to share contemplatively focused papers written by one another, which many did. After the gathering many volunteered to write a chapter for this book about some dimension of contemplative understanding and practice. With Margaret Benefiel's help, the book found a good publisher. Two participants graciously volunteered to edit the contents: Jessica Smith and Stuart Higginbotham. The chapters show both the special personal experience and the wisdom of the authors and the influence of their recent and historical contemplative mentors in the broader contemplative tradition. Together, I believe they offer a significant and timely contribution to evolving contemplative understanding and practice in our time.

Every reader I think will find some gems in these pages that not only will be personally stimulating but also give hope for the continuing expansion and enrichment of the contemplative reawakening in the hands of these and other young contemplative leaders today. Our conflicted, confused world so badly needs to become aware of and cultivate the deeper spiritual consciousness, the Spirit intimacy, that they have found in contemplative tradition and are called to foster for the world's well-being.

GROUNDING
IN PRACTICE

Contemplative Practices

THOMAS J. BUSHLACK

> *"Venerable sir, this is half of the holy life, that is,*
> *good friendship, good companionship, good*
> *comradeship."*
> *"Not so, Ananda! Not so, Ananda! This is the entire*
> *holy life, Ananda, that is, good friendship, good*
> *companionship, good comradeship."*
> —**The Connected Discourses of the Buddha**[1]

> *The devout Christian of the future will either be a*
> *"mystic," one who has experienced "something,"*
> *or will cease to be anything at all.*
> —**Karl Rahner, SJ**[2]

Friendships Forged in Silence

Those of us who gathered for the New Contemplative Exchange at St. Benedict's Monastery in August 2017 arrived from many parts of the globe, inspired by different teachers and expressions of contemplative practice. We each had our own goals, desires for our time together, and hopes for the future of contemplative Christian practice. The exchange had been structured as a blend of a conference-style gathering (with an emphasis upon working groups, goals, and objectives) and a retreat (with an emphasis on silence, contemplation, liturgy, and reflection). This brought to the surface a tension between goal-driven action and open-ended contemplation that led us in our initial dialogues to discern that any strategic actions or collaborative efforts in the future would emerge more from friendships forged in stillness than any grand organizational development schemes. We also noted the absence of a wider diversity of voices—those of our friends and colleagues who were not present—and we gave voice to our desire to prevent seeing our gathering as a limited or exclusive group (more on this below). We cultivated a conscious intention to develop solidarity and spiritual friendship with those present and absent, particularly with those voices not always acknowledged or heard in current discussions about contemplation. From that friendship we passionately committed to:

+ support each other in our leadership roles within our respective organizations around the globe

+ learn from each other's wisdom and experience

+ deepen our individual and collective contemplative practice

+ consider the implications of this "contemplative moment" for the Christian tradition as a whole, including for theology and pastoral praxis

+ consciously harness the healing energy of our practice toward genuine solidarity with those who were not adequately represented at our gathering, for the most vulnerable persons in our societies, and for the healing of the world and the common good of the planet and creation

These were lofty ideals; they emerged not from any hubris on our part or any sense that these tasks are *our* particular duty. Rather, they emerged as a shared calling, a responsibility toward authentic witness instilled by the encounter with the healing grace of the Holy Spirit in contemplative silence.

My task in this first chapter is to explore the nature of contemplative practice in a manner that can help us identify the contours of practices that delineate the contemplative experience while remaining broad enough to account for a real diversity of forms and expressions, both within and beyond the Christian tradition. To accomplish this goal, I begin with outlining what seem to me to be the essential components of a contemplative practice in general as well as across traditions. In the second section, I move into a consideration of distinctively Christian contemplative practices. Finally, in the third section I conclude with three suggestions for the future of contemplative Christianity. What I offer here is a big-picture perspective on contemplative practice based primarily upon my personal experience of more than two decades of regular contemplative prayer and meditation, and on my scholarship and encounters with other persons and texts in a variety of contemplative traditions.

I enter into this circle of friendship as a scholar-practitioner; I am both a committed practitioner of contemplative prayer and an academic trained in the disciplines of Christian theology and ethics. My practice is informed primarily by formative encounters with the Benedictine monastic tradition as a college student and subsequent involvement in Contemplative Outreach, and as a trustee of the Trust for the Meditation Process. In my early twenties I considered a vocation to the Benedictine monastic life, and eventually discerned a vocation as a lay oblate of St. Benedict through St. John's Abbey in Collegeville, Minnesota.[3] My embrace of Benedictine and contemplative spirituality as a lay person with a family and career places me in a unique position to teach and mediate the contemplative dimension of Christianity to others who have not had the same exposure to the classical practices and monastic sources that have provided a major—although not the only—communal context for fostering Christian contemplation over the centuries.

My personal practice is grounded in a meditative reading of scripture known as *lectio divina*,[4] a Latin phrase meaning "sacred" or "holy reading"; liturgical and sacramental participation in the Roman Catholic tradition; and Centering Prayer. My practice and teaching are also shaped by interspiritual encounters with persons, methods, and texts from a variety of contemplative traditions, especially Buddhist and yoga philosophies. I have also benefited greatly from the somatic dimension of hatha yoga, having received initiation from Dr. Stephen (Stoma) Parker of the Meditation Center in Minneapolis, Minnesota. The Himalayan lineage can be traced through Swami Rama (1925–1996) and Swami Veda Bharati (1923–2015).

My own experience with yogic practices echoes the broader contours of contemplative studies. The approach to contemplative practice shared by many emerging leaders is interspiritual, a term introduced by the Catholic monk and author Wayne Teasdale, who defines interspirituality simply as "the sharing of ultimate experiences across traditions."[5] Interspirituality is a term that evokes deep commitment to tradition and practice in a manner that is intentionally open to ecumenical and interfaith forms of encounter, friendship, and dialogue. Although sharing similarities with interfaith dialogue, interspirituality focuses more on the shared experience of and commitment to spiritual practices rather than intellectual discourse about differences in belief or doctrine, philosophy or theology.

I find this interspiritual approach helpful for remaining committed to my baptismal identity as a Roman Catholic in my theology and liturgical expression while also being open to theoretical and practical truths and insights received through the many contemplative traditions that make up the human community. In terms of practice, this interspiritual approach also underscores two core beliefs that guide my practice and scholarship: first, that progress and mature transformation in contemplative practice are best facilitated by stable commitment to a particular tradition and a worldview; and, second, that such stable commitment to a tradition does not narrow one's perspective toward a parochial, exclusivist, or judgmental worldview. Rather, an interspiritual stance affirms that moving deeply into one's "home" or "native" tradition can simultaneously open one to engage with the "other" in ways that affirm compassionate solidarity and respect genuine differences. This committed and open stance is both personally challenging and culturally prophetic in ways that I will explore in the latter part of this chapter.

Toward a Working Definition of *Contemplative Practice*

The attempt to articulate what is at the core of contemplative practice is a bit like the slippery attempt to pick up the bead of mercury from a broken thermometer. By its very nature, contemplative practice guides one toward a direct experience of the Ineffable, the Transcendent, to an encounter with God or the "divine milieu"[6]—to realms where words and human language reach the limits of their capacity to convey conceptual meaning. Therefore, the teacher-scholar Louis Komjathy provides sage advice by noting that "definitional parameters should be explored and discussed, rather than rigidly defined."[7]

Several years ago, I began to collect quotations from my devotional reading and research that seem to reflect something essential about the nature of contemplation.[8] Reflecting on this collection has become something of a contemplative exercise in itself. As a result of this informal research project I have begun to offer the following working definition of contemplation: Contemplation is a way of being present in awareness itself and a way of knowing by direct experience. It emerges from resting in a space of interior stillness of mind and body and opens toward a realization of union or oneness, universal love, or compassion.[9]

First, contemplation is *a way of being* that manifests within persons who cultivate a careful attention to both the interior and exterior dimensions of the present moment. The shift from "doing" toward "being" that occurs within contemplative practice may be one of the more confusing or difficult aspects of contemplation for people steeped in Western modes of existence. In the West we tend to reward action, doing, earning, and competition over being. The Catholic theologian and historian of Christian spirituality Bernard McGinn notes that contemplation is "a life-style, not an academic discourse";[10] neither is it a plan for personal success, growth, or development. Focusing on being over doing forms the entirety of the person and the way in which he or she is present to and engages with all reality. This includes one's interior life, that is, how one engages with thoughts, emotions, feelings, memories, the body and its sensations; and one's exterior life, that is, other persons, objects, the natural world, all of creation, and one's notion of God or Transcendence.

Mindfulness—described by the scientist, writer, and meditation teacher Jon Kabat-Zinn as "the intentional cultivation of nonjudgmental moment-to-moment awareness"[11]—is frequently upheld as foundational to practice, both for beginners and advanced practitioners, as the doorway into this new mode of being. In my experience, every contemplative tradition I have encountered emphasizes some form of mindful awareness (or a similar term) as an essential component of contemplative practice. This stance of suspended judgment and interior observation in an open space or field of awareness creates the ideal conditions within which a new way of being can emerge.

Second, contemplation is a way of *knowing by direct experience*. Regular practice guides the practitioner into a state of awareness in which the knower and that which is known are deeply relational. The psychologist Tobin Hart highlights how this contemplative knowing is a "third way of knowing" that "complements both the rational and the sensory [forms of knowing]"[12] It is important to note that contemplation *complements* other modes of knowing; it does not compete with or replace them. At the same time, it is not simply another mode of knowing alongside others. Contemplation exists in a different realm of consciousness in such a manner that it integrates and transcends other forms of knowing— not by surpassing those other modalities but by opening up to a completely different way of engaging reality. The Episcopal priest and prolific writer on contemplation Cynthia Bourgeault describes this as having an "'upgraded' operating system,"[13] an entirely new and holistic means of being, perceiving, and engaging with all reality. The theologian Barbara Holmes notes that within this contemplative knowing the practitioner recognizes implicitly that "there is an embodied knowing that exceeds the limits of rational thought."[14]

Third, this way of being and knowing *emerges from rest-*
ing in a space of interior stillness of mind and body and that
opens toward a realization of union or oneness, universal
love, and compassion. There are three aspects of this working definition's third part that I want to explore. To begin,
a contemplative way of being and knowing is something
that *emerges*. Stated alternatively, it is an emergent property
that arises—or bubbles up—into one's conscious awareness
from within regular contemplative practice. As an emergent
property, it is not something that can be summoned by will-
power or coerced into becoming. Paradoxically, it is quite
the opposite. Attempts to control or manipulate the experience causes contemplative knowing to dissipate like clouds
of mist dispersed in the winds of ego and self-will. When this
way of being and knowing does emerge, it flows effortlessly
out of the space of interior freedom cultivated through regular practice. It is the fruit of regular, disciplined commitment
to practice.

The manifestation of this emergent property is best facilitated by *resting in a space of interior stillness of mind and*
body. Contemplative traditions provide various practical
methods aimed at helping the practitioner still or calm what
the poet R. S. Thomas calls the "wild hawk of the mind,"[15]
or what Hart calls the "habitual chatter of the mind."[16] This
chatter acts as a kind of running commentary on our experience that keeps us in a state of distraction or fragmentation.
It becomes a subjectively colored layer of interpretation that
we impose upon reality—one that is influenced by all kinds
of personal and cultural biases, preferences, and preconceptions. The practitioner soon learns that the vast majority of
these preconceptions are false misconceptions that perpetuate
personal and collective suffering.

Contemplative practice provides a focal point for attention around which the practitioner learns to tether the wandering mind. The focal point itself is varied in different traditions and practices and may include, but is not limited to:

- focused, prayerful engagement with sacred or revealed texts

- working with the breath

- conscious bodily movement, such as in yoga, tai chi, martial arts, dance, or walking meditation; or conscious bodily stillness, such as in body scan meditation, yoga *nidra*, or assuming particular physical postures while meditating

- interior use or repetition of a sacred word or mantra

- singing or chanting of sacred texts

- rituals that bring one into direct encounter with transcendence within the natural world, such as Aboriginal or First Nation practices from around the globe

- in certain situations, externally imposed disciplines that are not consciously chosen, such as modern Africana contemplative traditions that emerged out of the experience of slavery[17]

This notion of contemplative being as an emergent property also underscores that the original, natural, or authentic human state includes an underlying clarity of awareness, an intimate being-in-relation that is innate to all human persons. This process is described eloquently in the following quote from Hari M. Sharma and Christopher Clark, who write from the Indian tradition of Ayurvedic healing:

The most fundamental reality is said to be completely subjective—an unbounded and eternal field of pure, abstract intelligence, or consciousness. This unified field is the home of all the laws of nature. What we see as the material world is, in reality, waves, or fluctuations, or impulses, of this non-material, underlying field of pure consciousness. What we ourselves are—or more exactly, what our minds and bodies are—is pure intelligence in motion. In the Vedic understanding, *if the human mind becomes still and pure enough, it can contact this pure field of consciousness* at the basis of the physical world. It can settle down to become directly aware of it.[18]

This general description of contemplation is also represented in figure 1 below.

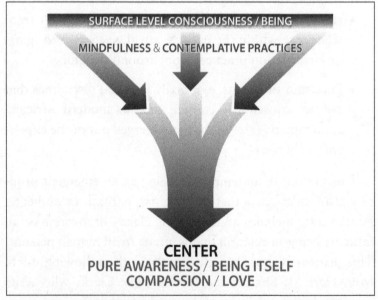

SURFACE LEVEL CONSCIOUSNESS / BEING

MINDFULNESS & CONTEMPLATIVE PRACTICES

CENTER
PURE AWARENESS / BEING ITSELF
COMPASSION / LOVE

Figure 1. The contemplative process[19]

Finally, contemplation *opens toward a realization of union or oneness, universal love, and compassion.* This relational, intimate texture of contemplative being is not something added onto an otherwise impersonal experience. Rather, it is integral to the process of contemplative transformation. Indeed, concrete expressions of love or compassion are a hallmark of authentic fidelity to contemplative practice. For the practitioner this loving quality of awareness is experienced as something both received from outside (with gratitude) and emanating out toward others and to all of reality (with loving-kindness). Thus, contemplative practice, if followed into its full expression, places one into a state of flow with a living Consciousness that is inherently loving, healing, and embracing of all that is.

This working definition suggests that any practices that facilitate the process of cultivating this kind of being present to awareness and of knowing or encountering reality by means of direct experience may be deemed contemplative. My second task is now to explore some of the ways contemplative practice manifests in the Christian tradition.

Christian Contemplative Practice: Friendship with God and Neighbor

Christian contemplative practices are best approached as a family of practices tethered together by shared commitment to cultivating an intimate relationship with the God who is revealed in scripture (the Hebrew Bible and the Christian New Testament), encountered in the person of Jesus Christ, and eternally present vis-à-vis the grace of the Holy Spirit. This intimate relationship is often described by Christian contemplatives as a mystical union with God, or, as Thomas Aquinas

(1225–1274 CE) preferred to state it, in friendship with God. I find it helpful to combine two distinct but related ways of describing Christian contemplation, one from Gregory the Great (540–604 CE), who defines it as "resting in God,"[20] and the other Fr. Thomas Keating, who describes it as "the Trinity dwelling in us."[21] Taken together, these descriptions point toward an interdependent, nondual, or mutual indwelling that suggests the possibility of awakening to our true union between human and divine—the human resting in divinity, and divinity dwelling in the human heart. One classic way of describing this mutual indwelling is "recollection," described by Teresa of Avila (1515–1582 CE) as a state in which "the soul collects its faculties together and enters within itself to be with its God."[22] The emphasis on "practice" highlights that this is not merely a theological abstraction but a real, embodied encounter between God and the human person that is transformative of the entire person.

The working definition I offered above regarding the broadest sense of contemplation specifically applies to Christian contemplative practice as well. The Christian contemplative tradition emphasizes how *being present in awareness itself* and *knowing reality by direct experience* includes awareness of and personal relationship with the Triune God who is revealed in scripture and in the person of Jesus Christ. In more theological terms, God is an intimate communion of three persons who exist as a trinity of God the Father, Jesus the Son, and the Holy Spirit (or the Creator, the Redeemer, and the Sanctifier, for those who prefer more gender inclusive language). The Christian tradition also emphasizes the manner in which contemplative transformation is the effect of God's action vis-à-vis grace, rather than a result of human effort or self-will. Christian contemplation is definitively not a self-help program. It is a program of continual and progressive self-surrender to divine transformation. In a distinctively Christian form of mindfulness, nonjudgmental, moment-to-moment awareness occurs within a dynamic relationship with this same God who is the very foundation of all that is.

The particular way of being that *emerges* in Christian practice is not a result of human effort but is rather a gift of grace. As St. Paul states, contemplation is received "because God's love has been poured into our hearts through the Holy Spirit that has been given to us" (Rom 5:5); it is a pure and freely offered gift of grace in which the contemplative joyfully delights, even amid struggle and suffering. Most of the activities we might think of as Christian contemplative practices are precisely those ways a practitioner learns to rest *in a space of interior stillness of mind and body* that facilitates a receptive state so that he or she is open to the divine presence and action. And finally, since "God is love" (1 Jn 4:8), and this love includes love of one's neighbor as oneself (see Matthew 22:37–39; Mark 12:30–31; and Luke 10:27), *the realization of union or oneness* with God is also an intimate encounter with a dynamic energy of *universal love or compassion* between and within all persons and being in existence.

In my experience the primary activity that occurs in contemplative practice is the letting go of all that stands between me and the realization of the fundamental oneness between me and God. One of the great insights provided by the anonymous fourteenth-century author of *The Cloud of Unknowing* is that God cannot be approached ultimately through the normal powers of the mind. Indeed, the author writes that "any thing that you think about is . . . between you and your God."[23] This suggests that the true nature of created reality itself is *already* one of union. Our attachments, biases, and selfish desires are what prevent us from knowing how deeply we are loved and immersed in this union. The late Fr. Joseph Boyle, former abbot of St. Benedict's Monastery, provided a lovely metaphor as he welcomed us to the monastery when he suggested that the valley in which the monastery resides is often experienced by guests like being held in the hand of God. The valley itself becomes a metaphor for the entire universe in the hand of God—guest resting in God; God dwelling within.

Figure 2. Held in the hand of God in Snowmass Valley (Photo: Thomas Bushlack)

With regular practice, the small sense of the separate and suffering "I," "self," or "ego" is slowly dissolved to the point of realizing that my usual sense of self is an illusion, until "it is no longer I who live, but it is Christ who lives in me" (Gal 2:20). Practice is our way of showing up and allowing God's grace to do its work of drawing us into an awareness of our mutual indwelling between us and our Creator.

I mentioned above that Christian contemplative practices are best approached as a family of practices tethered together by a shared commitment to an intimate relationship with Christ. On the one hand, we often associate contemplation with traditional images of meditation—sitting in stillness and an atmosphere of silence or quiet. This tendency was certainly represented in the way we practiced together in silent, sitting practice at the New Contemplative Exchange. In fact, data from a survey I administered to attendees indicated that the primary practice of 65 percent of those present was Centering Prayer; 35 percent practiced Christian Meditation, and 85 percent indicated *lectio divina* as their secondary form of practice.[24] On the other hand, we noted on the first day of our gathering that those of us invited were not fully representative of the broader diversity of forms and expressions of Christian practice.

Although we did have representation from a variety of minority perspectives, our group lamented a lack of even greater representation of diversity than what was present, as well as a fuller range of styles or forms of Christian contemplative practice. This kind of broader representation is important for honoring the rich diversity of practices and persons engaged in this contemplative moment for the Christian tradition.[25] As Barbara A. Holmes has indicated, Africana practices such as the ring shout, chanting, silent prayer in the hush arbors, dance, sacred harp, and shape-note singing, or being "slain in the spirit,"[26] can all point toward an inner contemplative space of interior stillness, solitude, and silence. Honoring the entire range of contemplative practice also helps purify the Christian tradition from a heavy tradition of "spiritual colonialism"[27] that privileges certain forms of (Eurocentric) contemplative expression over others. The teachings of

Holmes and the spiritual director and retreat leader Lerita Coleman Brown insist that for those who have been silenced, manifesting an awareness of our union with God and thus the embodiment that comes from such a transformed awareness in vocally and physically expressive forms is both contemplative and powerfully liberating. I experienced a similar kind of aha moment about the limits of my own preferred form of practice, as a trustee of the Trust for the Meditation Process, when listening to a presentation about mindfulness practice in the Minneapolis public schools. The presenters noted that some children who had experienced violence and trauma in their homes found that the simple act of closing their eyes in order to meditate can trigger fear and anxiety. They needed to adjust their teaching in order to honor a diversity of doorways into contemplative practice.

Figure 3. Seeking a wider circle of friendship (Photo: Thomas Bushlack)

Emerging Questions and Challenges

I cannot possibly capture the full range of experiences and expressions that make up Christian contemplative practice in this short chapter, nor can I outline all the questions and challenges that arise out of this contemplative moment for the church. Instead, I will conclude by offering three suggestions, each of which presents its own set of questions and challenges, which I will then explore very briefly. I hope these serve as a starting point for further dialogue, development, and challenge. As we give thanks for the foundational work of prior generations of teachers and leaders, future leaders of contemplative Christianity will need to pay attention to shepherding contemplative practices that are *embodied*, *pluralist*, and *integrative*.

As a religious tradition centered in the Incarnation—that is, the teaching that God assumed the form of a fully human body and walked on the earth in Jesus Christ—Christianity has a troubled history with the body (to put it mildly). Although historically Western approaches have tended to emphasize contemplation as an intellectual activity, today's practitioners, scholars, and teachers are increasingly attentive to how contemplative practice awakens fully embodied and socially situated persons to intimate communion with all that is. Cynthia Bourgeault emphasizes, for example, how Christian contemplation is a quality that emerges from placing "the mind in the heart."[28] The practitioner places his or her awareness both literally within the physical heart-space and metaphorically in the heart, understood as the spiritual center of the human person. Christian meditators also pay more attention to breath, posture, and mindful movement as essential and supportive dimensions to entering into interior stillness. A deepening appreciation for the embodied nature of contemplative practice can help all Christians remember that we are saved *in* the body, not *from* the body.

I mentioned at the beginning of this chapter that the committed and open stance of contemplation is both personally challenging and culturally prophetic. In order to express this reality, Christian contemplative practice is called to be pluralist. When I use the term *pluralist*, I do not mean the same thing as *pluralistic*. The latter term tends toward a kind of relativism in which all practices and methods are deemed equal, or reduced to a least common denominator. A pluralist perspective, on the other hand, recognizes a true historical, cultural, linguistic, and ethnic diversity of manifestations of contemplation.[29] In practice this means that Christian contemplation is ecumenical, that is, engaged in dialogical exchange within and between Christian denominations and groups; interspiritual, as described above; and affirming of a plurality of forms of expression or methods of practice.

Finally, Christian contemplative practice will also be integrative, especially with regard to integrating action and contemplation on behalf of justice. Christianity has a long tradition of reflection on the relationship between contemplation and action. In the Middle Ages there was a strong social distinction made between "contemplatives," vowed religious men and women living in monastic communities, and "the laity," those who work, raise families, and build up civil society. Many practitioners today recognize, however, that this is a limited, dualistic way to approach an integrative practice. Every committed contemplative has activities that he or she must accomplish; and every activist needs to be attentive to cherishing inner resources grounded in stillness and silence. An integrative contemplative practice looks to infuse the entirety of life with an undivided orientation of one's entire heart toward God, for "when I sit down and when I rise up; you discern my thoughts from far away" (Ps 139:2). Today's contemplatives are struggling to discern a call to live fully engaged in the sufferings and challenges of the world—including social injustices and harm to our environment—while bringing a contemplative desire for healing, integration, reconciliation, and friendship into the wounds of a broken world. We see this bearing fruit in a renewed appreciation for the spiritual and contemplative foundations of the civil rights movement for African Americans (especially in the life and writings of the theologian Howard Thurman), and in the spiritual struggles that have provided a major impetus for the growth of liberation theology in Latin America and its growth into a global theological phenomenon.[30] This is the prophetic witness that is the fruit of genuine contemplative transformation emerging from an encounter with a God who burns with "an almost fanatical love of justice."[31] This contemplative moment for Christianity will be (rightly) judged by whether or not we stand in solidarity—with our physical bodies—in the social spaces and in friendship with the wounded bodies and spirits of those most in need of justice, reconciliation, and healing.

Notes

1. Upaḍḍha Sutta (Saṃyutta Nikāya, Maggasaṃyutta 1.2). English translation from *The Connected Discourses of the Buddha: A Translation of the Saṃyutta Nikāya*, trans. Bhikkhu Bodhi (Boston: Wisdom Publications, 2000), 1524.

2. Karl Rahner, "Christian Living Formerly and Today," in *Theological Investigations VII*, trans. David Bourke (New York: Herder and Herder, 1971), 15.

3. An oblate is "a Christian who seeks God through a formal relationship with a particular monastic community. Oblates are men or women, lay or ordained, married or single, who seek to integrate the spirit of St. Benedict in their daily lives." "The Oblates of Saint John's Abbey," Saint John's Abbey, accessed April 11, 2018, http://www.saintjohnsabbey.org /monastic-life/oblates.

4. "Lectio Divina," Saint John's Abbey, accessed April 12, 2018, http:// www.saintjohnsabbey.org/monastic-life/oblates.

5. Wayne Teasdale, *The Mystic Heart: Discovering a Universal Spirituality in the World's Religions* (Novato, CA: New World Library, 1999). The term is also adopted by Rory McEntee and Adam Bucko, *The New Monasticism: An Interspiritual Manifesto for Contemplative Living* (Maryknoll, NY: Orbis Books, 2015).

6. This phrase was used by the French philosopher and Jesuit Pierre Teilhard de Chardin to capture the cosmic scope of the contemplative encounter with God; see especially *The Divine Milieu* (New York: Harper Perennial Modern Classics, 2001).

7. Louis Komjathy, *Introducing Contemplative Studies* (Hoboken, NJ: Wiley-Blackwell, 2017), 52.

8. Some of these citations are available at https://thomasjbushlack.com /favorite-quotes-contemplative-prayer-meditation-mindfulness.

9. I'm particularly grateful to my friend and colleague Dr. Tonia Bock for helping me refine this definition through a series of conversations and revisions.

10. Bernard McGinn, *The Essential Writings of Christian Mysticism* (New York: Modern Classics, 2006), xiv.

11. Jon Kabat-Zinn, "Mindfulness Meditation: What It Is, What It Isn't, and Its Role in Health Care and Medicine," in *Comparative and Psychological Study on Meditation*, ed. Y. Haruki, Y. Ishii, and M. Suzuki (Netherlands: Eburon, 1996), 161.

12. Tobin Hart, "Opening the Contemplative Mind in the Classroom," *Journal of Transformative Education* 2, no.1 (2004): 28; italics added for emphasis.

13. Cynthia Bourgeault, *The Heart of Centering Prayer: Nondual Christianity in Theory and Practice* (Boulder, CO: Shambhala Publications, 2016), 50.

14. Barbara A. Holmes, *Joy Unspeakable: Contemplative Practices of the Black Church* (Minneapolis: Fortress Press, 2004), 65.

15. Cited in Martin Laird, *Into the Silent Land: A Guide to the Christian Practice of Contemplation* (New York: Oxford University Press, 2006), 23.

16. Hart, "Opening the Contemplative Mind," 28.

17. See Holmes, *Joy Unspeakable,* especially chap. 3.

18. Hari M. Sharma and Christopher Clark, *Ayurvedic Healing: Contemporary Maharishi Ayurveda Medicine and Science*, 2nd ed. (London: Singing Dragon, 2012); italics added.

19. Graphic is courtesy of Valerie Boyd of BoyDesigns (boydesign@comcast.net).

20. Gregory the Great, prologue to *Moral Reflections on the Book of Job*, trans. Brian Kerns (Collegeville, MN: Cistercian Publications, 2014).

21. Thomas Keating, *Intimacy with God* (New York: Crossroad, 1994), 32.

22. Teresa of Avila, *The Way of Perfection*, ch. 28, no. 4; in *The Collected Works of Teresa of Avila*, trans. Kieran Kavanaugh and Otilio Rodriguez (Washington, DC: ICS Publications, 1980), 141.

23. *The Cloud of Unknowing*, chap. 5, no. 2. Translation cited in Bourgeault, *Heart of Centering Prayer,* 149.

24. See Thomas J. Bushlack and Tonia Bock, "Validating the 'Centering for Wisdom Assessment': Assessing the Role of Contemplative Practice in the Cultivation of Practical Wisdom," *Journal of Psychology and Theology* 46, no. 3 (April 3, 2018): 19n17.

25. I note in particular the work of Teresa Pasquale Mateus and the Mystic Soul Project (www.mysticsoulproject.com), Dr. Barbara A. Holmes (cited above), and Dr. Lerita Coleman Brown (peaceforhearts.com /about-me), among others.

26. Holmes, *Joy Unspeakable*, 21.

27. Komjathy, *Introducing Contemplative Studies*, 4.

28. She takes up this phrase from the *Philokalia*, a collection of classical spiritual texts in the Eastern Orthodox Churches. See Bourgeault, *Heart of Centering Prayer*, 53, and also 53–76.

29. One small, but highly significant, historical shift that would help in this decolonization process is to reimagine Christianity's history as emerging from a cultural context informed by North African, Middle Eastern, and Asian cultures, rather than viewing it through a later (and presumably inevitable) shift to a Eurocentric paradigm in the Middle Ages. It is here where Jesus walked the earth, and where Christian contemplative spirituality first took root in the rocky soil of the desert among the Desert Mothers and Fathers in the third and fourth centuries.

30. For example, see Gustavo Gutierrez, *We Drink from Our Own Wells: The Spiritual Journey of a People*, trans. Matthew J. O'Connell (Maryknoll, NY: Orbis Books, 1983).

31. Albert Einstein, "An Ideal of Service to Our Fellow Man," written for the radio show *This I Believe*, 1954, accessed May 21, 2018, https://thisibelieve.org/essay/16465.

The Value of Learning Contemplation in Community

SARAH BACHELARD

In a café near you, wherever you are in the Western world, I warrant you're likely to find a poster or postcard picturing a poised and flexible-looking younger woman. Sometimes depicted in silhouette, sometimes gazing calmly toward you, she sits cross-legged against a background of blue sky or lush rain forest, radiating peace, togetherness, and a sense of having all the time in the world. "Meditation classes," the caption reads, "7 p.m. on Tuesdays; $180 for a six-week course." It looks so inviting, so de-stressing—just exactly what you need, a bit of "me" time.

Contemplative advertising has come quite a way, it seems, since the forbidding opening lines of the fourteenth-century treatise *The Cloud of Unknowing*:

> Whoever you are possessing this book, know that I charge you with a serious responsibility, to which I attach the sternest sanctions that the bonds of love can bear. It does not matter whether this book belongs to you, whether you are keeping it for someone else, whether you are taking it to someone, or borrowing it; you are not to read it, write or speak of it, nor allow another to do so, unless you really believe that he is a person deeply committed to follow Christ perfectly.[1]

And with that—bang—there goes the business model!

The juxtaposition of these "texts" addressed to would-be contemplatives highlights a cluster of questions, even tensions, involved in the contemporary communication of a contemplative way. These include issues to do with discernment of spiritual "fitness" for contemplative prayer, questions about the risk of spiritual commodification and its effect on spiritual growth, the relationship between egoic satisfaction and self-transcending faith, and the question—ultimately—of how isolated individuals become persons-in-relation.

My focus in this chapter is the value of learning contemplation in community. Traditionally, it was taken for granted that contemplative formation required being in relationship with a tradition, a teacher, and a community of practice. Yet such a view sits uneasily with that postcard image where a self-contained course is marketed to a self-sufficient individual, with no further commitment presupposed or demanded. Does the traditional view still hold? And if so, what implications does this have for the renewal of contemplative practice and the vocation of contemplative communities today? My focus in what follows will be on the Christian tradition, but I suspect similar issues may arise for the contemporary teaching of contemplation by other traditions as well.

Learning Contemplation

For much of Christian history, neophytes were warned that the way of contemplative prayer is not for everyone. *The Cloud of Unknowing*, as we have seen, begins in minatory fashion and goes on to specify in some detail those who shouldn't even think about it: "worldly gossips, flatterers, the scrupulous, talebearers, busybodies, and the hypercritical," as well as "the merely curious, educated or not. They may be good people by the standards of the active life," the writer concedes, "but this book is not suited to their needs."[2]

Who then is called to this way? The anonymous writer of *The Cloud of Unknowing* thinks this question needs careful discernment, and comes back to it in its final chapter. Someone drawn to the contemplative way must "examine himself" to see that he has done all he can to "purify his conscience of deliberate sin according to the precepts of the Holy Church and the advice of his spiritual father."[3] Then, more positively, he must consider how strongly he is drawn to this way—"if his conscience leaves him no peace in any exterior or interior work" unless his principal concern is the work of contemplative prayer, then "it is a sign that God is calling him to this work. But if these signs are lacking, I assure you, he is not."[4]

Some nine centuries earlier, John Cassian had said much the same. His *Conferences* on prayer emphasized the necessity of basic integrity—we must "unload all our vices and rid our souls of the wreck and rubble of passion"[5]—as well as the discernment that some deepened commitment to contemplation is being evoked in the spiritual seeker.[6]

In this regard, a remarkable feature of the recent contemplative renewal in Christianity is the widespread promulgation and ready accessibility of the teaching, and the understanding that, far from being the preserve of the practiced religious, contemplation may in fact constitute a point of entry to faith. John Main seems to have realized early in his teaching of Christian meditation that it was a practice of prayer that could be taught with few explicit preconditions and that it answered to a broadly felt sense of hunger for meaning in the modern world. In foundational writings for the World Community for Christian Meditation, he writes,

We are trying to share, as widely as we can, the tradition of Christian meditation. We hold the conviction
in our Community here that all the spiritual riches
of the New Testament, the full riches of what Christ
came to proclaim, are available for each of us if only
we can enter into his experience.[7]

In a similar vein, Frs. William Meninger, Basil Pennington, and Thomas Keating said they developed the practice of
Centering Prayer in response "to the Vatican II invitation to
revive the contemplative teachings of early Christianity and
present them in updated formats," with a view to their general availability.[8]

Does this mean the traditional caution in transmitting
the way of contemplation has been revealed to be spuri-
ous and so abandoned altogether? To the extent that reti-
cence in making this way generally known was entangled
with assumptions about the superiority of the contemplative
over the active life, and of the monastic or clerical over the
lay estate, it is clear there has been a notable democratiz-
ing of contemplative prayer. All are invited into the fullness
and depth of Christian life and, for the modern masters, all
that is required for anyone to embark on this deeper journey is to begin. The tradition of meditation, writes Main,
is "available for you and me. The only thing that is necessary is that we enter into it by beginning the practice."[9]
For Main, anyone who seeks out this teaching and begins to
practice it can be presumed to have the "hunger and humility," the yearning for "direct, personal experience of God"
that are the signs of true "calling" to contemplative work
enjoined by Cassian and *The Cloud of Unknowing* as its
necessary precondition.[10]

It is important to note that the traditional caution was not just about keeping meditation as the preserve of a supposed elite. It was also to do with awareness of spiritual risk in this way of prayer. Elements of this risk include the unsettling of self and God images and so a sense of radical disorientation,[11] dangers of self-delusion as to one's progress or of despair at prayer's aridity, the risk of spiritual self-consciousness and imagining oneself unduly special, and the possibility that one might spend years in pious "wool-gathering," going nowhere in particular.[12]

The concern that would-be contemplatives should have arrived at a degree of spiritual maturity, stability, and capacity for discernment is connected to the particular challenges of the way itself. And it's in this context, I think, that we may recognize the value—indeed, the necessity—of learning contemplation in community. Thomas Merton expressed this as starkly as any:

> The most dangerous man in the world is the contemplative who is guided by nobody. He trusts his own visions. He obeys the attractions of an interior voice but will not listen to other men. He identifies the will of God with anything that makes him feel, within his own heart, a big, warm, sweet interior glow. The sweeter and the warmer the feeling is the more he is convinced of his own infallibility.[13]

Less polemically but in a similar vein, Main saw the significance of meditating in community in terms of the encouragement to disciplined practice over time, as well as its engendering of a proper sense of humility and accountability in practitioners. In particular, he thought the community of meditators helped inculcate a sense of the ordinary, daily nature of this way of prayer with its radically transforming power that manifests not essentially in peak "spiritual" experiences but in the expansion of one's patience, mercy, compassion, and truth as proved in one's relationships with others.[14]

But exactly what kind of community is called for and called forth here? How in practice does this work? To explore this question, I need first to say a little more about the work of contemplation itself—what it is that we are seeking to learn and share.

The Work of Contemplation

From a Christian point of view, the great mystery that undergirds our contemplative endeavor is that God is given and endlessly self-giving. The intention of our practice is simply to bring us to the place where we may receive, where we may realize our communion with the source of our life and discover its nature as love. To pray as Christ prayed, "to be contemplative as Christ is contemplative," the former archbishop of Canterbury Rowan Williams says, "is to be open to all the fullness that the Father wishes to pour into our hearts."[15]

Becoming receptive to this gift calls for stillness and a degree of self-less attention. The theologian Beatrice Bruteau writes,

> [the] various devices for getting meditation started are all just ways of organizing our total consciousness, our whole mind and heart and soul, and making them hold still and pay attention, without being drawn away by other concerns, long enough to open themselves to the immense reality of the presence of God. Experiencing the presence and reality of God is what it is all about.[16]

And the point of this is not, as Williams goes on to insist, "because we are in search of some private 'religious experience' that will make us feel secure or holy." Rather, it is because "in this self-forgetting gazing towards the light of God in Christ we learn how to look at one another and at the whole of God's creation."[17]

Contemplation, in other words, is about being so dispossessed of our agendas, our anxieties, our way of seeing things, that we may come to share the mind of Christ—to be sourced where he is sourced, see as he sees, love as he loves. "We leave self behind," writes Main, "in order to find our enduring reality, to find ourselves one with the one with whom Jesus was one."[18]

Significantly, this makes clear that the value of learning contemplation in community is not merely instrumental, helpful for guarding against spiritual "risk" and for encouraging perseverance and discipline. Rather, contemplation itself creates community. It transforms us from fearful, self-protective, isolated individuals into persons open to God and so increasingly to one another. The more we experience ourselves receiving and resting in God's self-giving love for us, the more we discover ourselves simply loving one another and the world around us, desiring to care and serve.[19] And it is in fact the birth of this community of love that witnesses to and makes manifest the reality we contemplate, that proves (as it were) our deepening communion with the love—which is to say, the Trinitarian life—of God.

This truth is not in the least gainsaid by the fact that some contemplatives are called to live in solitude. Rather, it explains why even solitaries are traditionally attached to a community and a spiritual guide, their prayer offered as gift in service of others.[20] It does suggest, however, that a commodified, self-containing practice of meditation is a parody, an ulti-mately self-defeating simulacrum of the real thing. Of course, it is possible that we can start in one place and be drawn to another; we can begin disconnected from community with our privatized six-week course and yet find ourselves embarked on an increasingly self-dispossessing journey, a journey from isolation to communion. But if this possibility is really to be enabled, there needs to be wise guides, communities of con-templative practice and encouragement to join the company of pilgrims. Which brings us back to the question of what kind of community is called for and called forth by the con-templative way.

The Value of Contemplative Community

There are numbers of Christian contemplative communities now in existence. For many contemporary practitioners, the World Community for Christian Meditation and Contempla-tive Outreach have been profoundly important teachers, and meditation groups organized by and linked to them consti-tute a global network of practice. In addition, there are many other centers, networks, and worshipping communities, as well as emerging communities of contemplative practice based in or attached to older monastic foundations, cathe-drals, and parishes.[21] Such communities are local and online, residential and dispersed, vowed and nonvowed. They are often ecumenical and sometimes interfaith or interspiritual.

Mostly there is a core practice of silent prayer or medita-tion, but other contemplative practices are engaged to vary-ing extents. These may include *lectio divina*; bodily prayer such as yoga, tai chi, or Systema; chanting; contemplation of the natural world; reflection; pilgrimage; iconography; and art. The way of contemplative prayer is being brought into connection and conversation with a wide range of concerns, including the arenas of ecology, social action, leadership, business, health care, and more. Such diversity and emergence are signs of how a contemplative perspective transforms our sense of the whole of life and calls forth the desire for integration and reconciliation in every dimension.

In all this, however, there are challenges in forming contemplative communities capable of calling and sustaining people seriously on the way of transforming prayer and deepening faith. In what follows, I want to touch on two that particularly exercise me.

The first challenge concerns spiritual discipline. In almost every teaching he gave, Main insisted that if you really want to learn contemplation, if you really want to meditate, you must be faithful to a twice-daily practice and to the teaching itself. This faithfulness is not essentially about perfecting a particular method of prayer but yielding yourself wholeheartedly and without remainder to a way that takes you beyond yourself.[22] It is this discipline of self-transcending faith "that leads to personal transformation," and it is for this reason, Main says, that you cannot just do a "bit of meditation. If you want to meditate then you have to place it in a central position in your life."[23] Everything must come to be oriented around and in harmony with the practice.

Well, even Main found that this call to radical seriousness and discipline met at times with resistance and the charge of rigidity,[24] and this is true in my experience also. Partly, presumably, this is about the assertion of what the philosopher and novelist Iris Murdoch memorably called the "fat, relentless ego,"[25] which resists any perceived threat to its autonomy and momentary gratification. Partly, it may also be about the readiness of particular individuals and the time it takes to begin. But I wonder if some of this resistance is connected to dynamics internal to the contemplative renewal in our day.

Many drawn to contemplation are moving away from the institutional church and more conventional stages of faith.[26] They may also be reacting to experiences of "bad religion": fundamentalist or controlling churches, patronizing clergy, and corrupt ecclesial hierarchies. Given this, it can be a delicate matter as to how to teach the discipline of meditation and speak of the necessary surrender to the authority of the practice while offering genuine, noncoercive hospitality and the freedom to be. There's a tension between taking seriously people's call to spiritual "adulthood" and their necessarily personal engagement with the journey of transformation while recognizing the fact that this journey can be blocked or slowed by self-deception and self-will. It is a tension not always easy to name or address, particularly in an emerging contemplative community.

A second and related issue concerns the question of commitment to common or shared spiritual life. I have said that authentic contemplative practice naturally leads to community, and the concept of community has a warm place in our cultural imaginary—people like the idea of it and say they want it. But when it comes down to it, to what extent are we willing to commit and what are we prepared to sacrifice for its realization in our midst? And what constitutes the nature of true spiritual community in any case? In a monastic setting, there's a clear and explicit commitment to a rule of life and the sheer fact of physical proximity, though even here there's no guarantee of a real sharing of life and love.[27] But in nonresidential and nonvowed contemplative communities, things are significantly more ambiguous.

As I've reflected on the question of forming and nurturing contemplative community, it seems to me there are two poles that must be held in tension. On the one hand, there needs to be at least some members of the community who give of themselves to be there consistently, to grow in prayer and faith, to create together a context for encounter and transformation. On the other hand, there needs to be sufficient freedom within and between members of the community that people can participate in what is for them at that time the right way. Without this freedom, there is no genuine hospitality, no respecting the mystery of each person and the uniqueness of their unfolding journey toward wholeness. Yet in practice, this is not an easy tension to discern.

In a recent call for the renewal of the "deep structures" of Christian community, the Orthodox Christian writer Rod Dreher advocates "putting the life of the church first, even if you have to keep your kid out of a sports program that schedules the games during your church's worship services, . . . [and being prepared to sacrifice] attendance at events if they conflict with church."[28] I find myself uneasy with what seems here like an overly prescriptive conception of what true community must look like and require while being aware that in a culture like ours there is a real question about how to nourish communities that are more than gatherings of convenience.

These challenges in forming contemplative communities are by no means exhaustive or unique to our time. It is clear, for example, that St. Benedict knew all about the need to balance gentleness and rigor in relation to each person's needs and proclivities.[29] Perhaps, however, they are heightened by the democratization of contemplation and the flattening of spiritual hierarchies,[30] as well as by the pervasive impact of a consumer culture that encourages us to make our spiritual commitments fit into our schedules, and to react against anything that seems to limit our choices or freedom.

Yet notwithstanding (or perhaps because of) these difficulties, it seems to me that the formation of contemplative communities is of vital significance today. This is not only so there are contexts for learning and deepening the practice of contemplation. It is also so that a "body" of contemplative practice and consciousness is present in the life of the church and the world. Because, however gradually, our contemplative practice does change us. It creates space and silence within us, and so the capacity for more generous listening to God, ourselves, and one another. It leads us to become clearer about the difference between discerning and deciding, and so more able to engage in real conversation and reflection, and to bear unresolvedness over time until a deeper truth emerges. This, in turn, helps liberate us from the need to be driven by the perceived urgencies of the moment or to look busy and successful, and to be content instead to wait on the unfolding of call and response.

Where a contemplative community is learning to live together in this spirit, out of this experience, it constitutes a powerful witness and invitation to the possibility of living responsive to and trusting in the presence and action of God. Such a community is sacramental, incarnating a Christic way of being and belonging that is wholehearted and committed, yet compassionate, relaxed, and humane. It is prophetic in that it helps makes visible and so challenges destructive dynamics in the reigning culture.

The existence of such communities makes a real difference in the midst of a church increasingly obsessed with its own survival and looking "unhappily like so many purely human institutions, anxious, busy, competitive and controlling,"[31] and too often tending toward fundamentalism or sectarianism in reaction to the perceived depredations of secularism. It makes a difference, too, in a world where fear, envy, and greed undermine a sense of and commitment to the common good while shallow and dehumanizing political, media, and advertising cultures distort our vision and desire. We need to be able to imagine and participate in another way, and this is what contemplative communities can experience and open up for others.

And perhaps it is the very willingness to live with and through the challenge of forming and sustaining such communities in our culture that is part of how we become who we are called to be. Our prayer draws us, individually and communally, into the broad place of the freedom of the Spirit. This can help us navigate between tendencies to excessive rigor on the one hand and ill-discipline on the other, between oppressive communal conformity and taken-for-granted consumerist individualism. In this process, we may learn how truly to become "members one of another," how truly to care for each other's good and discover our part in that.

Contemplative practice transforms us into persons-in-relation. It opens the door to the possibility of authentic community. Exactly what that looks like in different places and for different groups is not laid down in advance. But in societies suffering destructive ideological, racial, and economic divisions and a pervasive sense of anxiety, threat, and siege, persons formed by prayer and community to practice deep listening, hospitality, and trust are surely our main hope of reconciliation and renewal. This, then, is the value of learning contemplation in community and the value of learning to be contemplative communities, open to the Spirit's leading and the increase of our love.

Notes

1. *The Cloud of Unknowing*, ed. William Johnston (New York: Image Books, 1996), 35.

2. *Cloud of Unknowing*, 35–36.

3. *Cloud of Unknowing*, 132.

4. *Cloud of Unknowing*, 133.

5. John Cassian, *Conferences*, trans. Colm Luibheid (Mahwah, NJ: Paulist Press, 1985), 9.2.

6. Cassian, *Conferences* 10.4, 10.8.

7. John Main, *Moment of Christ: Prayer as the Way to God's Fullness*, ed. Laurence Freeman (Norwich, UK: Canterbury Press, 2010), 19.

8. "History of Centering Prayer," Contemplative Outreach, accessed March 24, 2018, https://www.contemplativeoutreach.org/history -centering-prayer.

9. Main, *Moment of Christ*, 77.

10. John Main, *Monastery Without Walls: The Spiritual Letters of John Main*, ed. Laurence Freeman (Norwich, UK: Canterbury Press, 2006), 10.

11. This necessary unmasking of our false images of God and its disorienting effect is memorably characterized in Cassian's account of the old monk Sarapion. *Conferences* 10.3.

12. John Main speaks in this regard of the *pax perniciosa*, the pernicious peace, and "false piety, holy floating." *Monastery Without Walls*, 41–42.

13. Thomas Merton, *New Seeds of Contemplation* (New York: New Directions, 2007), 194–95.

14. "When people ask how they can tell if they are making progress in meditation, since they are not supposed to analyse or evaluate the actual time of meditation, the answer is: your life." Main, *Monastery Without Walls*, 16.

15. Rowan Williams, *The Archbishop of Canterbury's Address to the Thirteenth Ordinary General Assembly of the Synod of Bishops on the New Evangelization for the Transmission of the Christian Faith*, Dr. Rowan Williams 104th Archbishop of Canterbury (website), October 10, 2012,

sec. 6, http://rowanwilliams.archbishopofcanterbury.org/articles.php /2645/archbishops-address-to-the-synod-of-bishops-in-rome.

16. Beatrice Bruteau, *Radical Optimism: Practical Spirituality in an Uncertain World* (Boulder, CO: Sentient Publications, 2002), 54.

17. Williams, *Address to the Synod of Bishops*, sec. 7.

18. Main, *Monastery Without Walls*, 17.

19. Cf. Bruteau, *Radical Optimism*, 103.

20. Writes Merton, "The only justification for a life of deliberate solitude is the conviction that it will help you to love not only God but also other men." *New Seeds of Contemplation*, 52.

21. Examples of the former include the Center for Action and Contemplation, Shalem Institute for Spiritual Formation, the Taizé and Iona communities, Gravity: Center for Contemplative Activism, Metanoia of Vermont, Benedictus Contemplative Church, and various new monastic communities. Examples of the latter include the oblate communities of monastic orders and emerging contemplative parishes, such as Grace Episcopal Church in Gainesville, Georgia.

22. For John Main, the practice that corresponds with this total self-yielding is that of saying the mantra without ceasing and "until you can no longer say it." *Monastery Without Walls*, 21. Centering Prayer suggests a different relationship to the mantra. However, the underlying intention of both is the same—to surrender egoic self-consciousness so as to be drawn into the stream of love that flows eternally between Jesus and his Father.

23. Main, *Moment of Christ*, 59.

24. See Main, *Monastery Without Walls*, 20–21.

25. Iris Murdoch, *The Sovereignty of Good* (London: Routledge, 1996), 52.

26. Richard Rohr has helpfully characterized nine stages of faith or levels of development. *The Naked Now: Learning to See as the Mystics See* (New York: Crossroad, 2009), 163–66.

27. See Thomas Merton, *Conjectures of a Guilty Bystander* (Tunbridge Wells, UK: Burns & Oates, 1995), 174.

28. Rod Dreher, *The Benedict Option: A Strategy for Christians in a Post-Christian Nation* (New York: Sentinel, 2017), 125. To my mind, the

title's invocation of the notion of "strategy" is part of what signals something amiss in the spirit of this book.

29. See, for example, *The Rule of Benedict*, trans. Anthony C. Meisel and M. L. del Mastro (New York: Image Books, 1975), chaps. 2 and 34. Before St. Benedict's time, there is the endearing story of the Desert Father Abba Poeman, to whom some "righteous brethren" complain about others who "irritatingly nod off during the liturgy." Poeman replies, "For my part when I see a brother who is dozing, I put his head on my knees and let him rest." Cited in Mark McIntosh, *Discernment and Truth: The Spirituality and Theology of Knowledge* (New York: Cross-road, 2004), 141.

30. Merton, *New Seeds of Contemplation*, 197.

31. Williams, *Address to the Synod of Bishops*, sec. 15.

Celebrating the
Discipline of Prayer

SICCO CLAUS

Whenever I give a lecture or course on prayer, I feel a little unease when I must bring up the topic of discipline, of commitment. John Main, whose views on prayer I usually share during such occasions, emphasizes that one needs to meditate *twice daily*, *every day of our life*, for *twenty to thirty minutes*.[1] Although after some years the rhythm of twice-daily meditations has been more or less established in my life, it is not particularly hard for me to remember my sense of fright when this particular instruction came to me for the first time. I recall that I instantly started to play it down. Moreover, if somebody would have said that discipline in fact is closely related to celebration, I would have thought this person to be a bit disturbed. Yet there *is* a deep relationship between commitment and celebration, a relationship I will explore in more detail. I hope to show that it is exactly my growing sense of this intimate connection that has kept me going over the years. In doing so, I will not shy away from questioning whether this specific approach of commitment isn't completely outdated given the secular age, as the philosopher Charles Taylor has dubbed the times we live in.[2]

In what is to follow, I hope to illuminate the relationship between the discipline of meditation, both in the wider sense of practice and in the limited sense of determination on the one hand and celebration on the other. I will explain the teaching I have received: the practice of Christian Meditation as promoted by Main. Focusing on the practicalities of this practice will soon reveal that the explication of the wider religious conceptual framework that comes with it cannot be omitted, for this context provides the ultimate reason why engaging oneself in this practice as well as to keep going is so worthwhile. This ultimate reason I will call "the festive dimension of prayer." While explicating why celebration in the end constitutes prayer, we will, however, also quickly stumble upon a not-so-festive dimension. This dimension makes discipline in the more restricted sense a necessity. Yet the promise is that even this noncelebrational element in the end will be transformed into feast. Given the cultural condition in which Main's teaching on meditation finds itself, this exploration would be incomplete if the secular framework and its specific sensitivities would be ignored. I will therefore end my chapter by mentioning some points I see as relevant when teaching contemplation from the Christian tradition with what Charles Taylor calls "the immanent frame."[3]

Discipline with Regards to a Discipline

John Main's teaching on prayer is very simple. Still in his twenties, working in diplomatic service in Malaya, he met a Hindu Swami who ran a temple and social center just outside Kuala Lumpur.[4] Main was instantly impressed by the calm and peaceful wisdom of the man.[5] After having discussed the spiritual practices both of them followed, Main decided he wanted to learn meditation as the swami practiced it. He meditated with him once a week for about eighteen months.

The swami emphasized that, in the end, everything comes down to interiorly saying one's prayer word for twenty to thirty minutes, twice daily.

After returning to England, Main taught law at Trinity College, Dublin. In his thirties he felt called to become a Benedictine monk, after the death of his nephew stirred up questions for him about life and death and the meaning of life that couldn't be brought to rest in a conventional way anymore. He realized his twice-daily meditations were the most important thing in his entire existence. However, when he entered the monastery, he was asked to end his meditation practice. This is not a Christian way of praying, he was told. Later in his life he became headmaster of a Benedictine school in Washington, DC. Here a young man interested in Christian mysticism came to the monastery to be taught about Christian mysticism. Reading a book of Dom Augustine Baker (1571–1641) together with his pupil, Main discovered striking parallels between the form of meditation he learned in the East and the type of pure, spiritual prayer referred to by this seventeenth-century English Benedictine author.

Main points out that Baker's words in turn also made him aware of the emphasis St. Benedict places on the classical spiritual John Cassian's teaching on prayer. It stimulated him to seriously read Cassian (360ʾ–435) for the first time. To his astonishment, Cassian, the author who collected the wisdom of the Desert Mothers and Fathers and brought it to the West, recommends the use of a *formula*, a single short phrase to achieve the receptivity necessary for prayer. Cassian recommends repeating the phrase "God, come to my aid; Lord, come to rescue me." He believes this *formula* to be an outstanding tool to help one lay aside thought and restrict the mind to the poverty of this verse. In this recommendation,

Main sees if not the same then a similar teaching as the instruction he received from the swami.

Another strong parallel Main discovers between the Hindu swami's teaching on meditation and the Christian tradition of prayer is in the fourteenth-century text *The Cloud of Unknowing*. This volume, written by an anonymous author, recommends the use of a one-syllable prayer word to focus our naked will on God. Centering Prayer, a contemplative practice developed by the Cistercian monks William Meninger, Basil Pennington, and Thomas Keating[6] draws its inspiration primarily from this text.[7]

While both Cassian and *The Cloud of Unknowing* mention the importance of the continuous use of a prayer word, there are also dissimilarities between the instruction of these two spiritual authors and Main's. Main stresses the continuous repetition of the prayer word during two formal moments of prayer within a clearly defined time frame: twenty to thirty minutes. Cassian, however, speaks about the need to use the prayer word during the whole of one's day, in the process of "keeping up continual recollection of God," in particular during specific moments of spiritual temptation.[8] *The Cloud of Unknowing* remains silent about the precise context in which the prayer word is advisable. Although it is clear that the setting is contemplation, this doesn't indicate a clearly defined practice.

Precisely this practice of repeating a prayer word for the whole time of the period of prayer, twice daily, requires discipline. Main is well aware of this, as he told a group of monks, specifically the Cistercians of Gethsemani Abbey, the monastery in which Thomas Merton used to live: "But don't let me mislead you. Actually to say the word morning and evening, day in and day out, winter and summer, whether you feel like it or don't feel like it, all this requires a good deal of grit, determination, and steel in the spine."[9] Although he talks to monks here, overseeing the whole of his texts, Main certainly didn't believe the relevance of this type of prayer would be restricted to the life of professional pray-ers. On the contrary, time and time again he emphasizes this prayer form as suitable and relevant for *all* Christians. Yet given his stress on the need for discipline, for "steel in the spine," we are in need for a good explanation why to engage in such a demanding practice. Moreover, hasn't the idea of prayer as celebration silently disappeared behind the horizon by now?

Theologically Interpreting Discipline

As a way to motivate his students to meditate daily, meditation teacher Jon Kabat-Zinn tells us we should make sure we weave our parachute every day, rather than leave it to the time we have to jump out of the plane. Obviously Kabat-Zinn's emphasis on discipline is a clear parallel with Main's stress upon the need for building in the discipline of meditation in your daily life. But when attending a mindfulness course some time ago, I couldn't help thinking, "What if I am not in a plane and moreover don't feel the slightest inclination to get into one within a reasonable time frame? Then all the weaving that needs to be done is rather useless." What is more, it strikes me that many people I know who attend a mindfulness course sooner or later stop their daily practice. The reason they had for starting with it, usually an overload of stress, has disappeared and the risk that such stressful situations might reappear soon becomes rather abstract.

Main presents a totally different kind of explanation why meditation, why deep prayer is important. The palette of metaphors and concepts he employs to express the ultimate reason why one should engage in this practice is very rich, hence I will need to limit myself. One of the ways he expresses it is that in meditation we can fully receive the gift of our being. Here the festive dimension immediately comes to the fore: apparently our condition ultimately is *not* something that needs to be protected by parachutes but is a condition of "givenness." Moreover, isn't it true that an important characteristic of a celebration is precisely the sharing and receiving of gifts? "Our awakening is," Main argues, ". . . the awareness of our participation in the life of God, of God as the source of our personhood, the very power by which we are enabled to accept His gift of our being. It is therefore a free response, an utterly personal communication, a free acceptance."[10] Since the Christian view is that we don't believe that creation is a one-time event sunk in the past but a *continuous creation*, we are invited to receive *daily* this gift of our being.

Another, even deeper way of viewing what is at stake in our daily meditation practice is a process of divinization, that is, we somehow start to participate in a very intimate way in the life of the Divine: "We come to appreciate, in the reverent silence of our prayer, that we are infinitely holy as temples of God's own Spirit. We learn to remember who we are, and that our vocation is to look upon and contemplate the Godhead itself and thus to be ourselves divinized."[11] Thus seen from Main's theology of prayer, it is not only that we accept the gift of our created being through silent prayer but also a fundamental transformation takes place dubbed divinization. Yet what does it mean to become divinized? Although Main, fully grounded in the tradition of apophatic theology, is well aware of the mysteriousness of it, he points out, "It is our capacity to love and to be rooted in love that is the essence of our divinization."[12]

Here we find the festive dimension of the discipline of meditation in an even more profound sense. Apart from the fact that we receive the gift of our being, we can also give ourselves back in love. In this very process we share in the giving and receiving that takes place in the heart of the divine mystery itself, which is the festive core of the Trinity. In our daily prayer we are invited to become aware of, to awaken to, the fact that *this* is our ultimate reality. Is this not an existing perspective and therefore a very good reason to meditate at least twice daily?

The Not-So-Festive Dimension of Discipline

We must pause a moment here and ask ourselves, even if one accepts this perspective in faith, why is it often far from easy to meditate? Part of the answer is that so far, I have left out from the picture the One who is the reason why I dare to put this explanation of why we should meditate in front of you.

In his famous book on mystical theology, the scholar Mark A. McIntosh points out, "If we think for a moment of the Christian Neoplatonism of Dionysius or Eriugena, Bonaventure, Eckhart, or Jan van Ruusbroec—all quite various in formulation—there is a familiar and unmistakable pattern involved: the procession of all things from their eternal being in God into created existence, and the return of all into blissful unity with God."[13] Clearly Main's way of formulating his theological justification of meditation is a contemporary expression of precisely this tradition.

McIntosh, however, revealingly and crucially adds to this picture that "the *pivotal turning point* in this . . . dynamic is a concrete historical event: the life, death, and resurrection of

Jesus."[14] How does Main see all this? Affirming the *unveiling through veiling* moment of the Jesus event, he argues, "The language we use to express this mystery [of Christ], the greatest and fundamental mystery of the human race and of all time, is pathetically inadequate—as the theological controversies down through the centuries have shown. No language or concept or metaphor can express the mystery of Christ, because *Christ is the full embodiment of God* and there can be no adequate expression of God except his own self-expression."[15] In other words, Main recognizes in Jesus Christ this pivotal turning point in the divine dynamic that McIntosh, in line with the great mystical theologians, believes to be at work in history.

One's faith in Jesus as the hinge of the process of going forth and returning to God sheds a particular light on why it is often hard to remain faithful to our daily prayer practice, even if we have the fascinating vision painted above in front of us. A Christian is aware of the invitation to participate in the loving, self-sharing dynamic of the Trinity *through* the historical life of Jesus. This life, however, also makes painfully clear that existing in the mode of giving and receiving love in our world isn't always appreciated. We as human beings have managed to create a world in which such a life ends up hanging on a cross. Unless we think that if we would have been around, the horrific tragedy of the Cross wouldn't have happened, this very fact remains an invitation to reflect on what "for God's sake" went wrong in the most profound sense of the word.

For Main, reflecting the mainstream of the Christian tradition, what went wrong was that we got stuck in the illusion that anything can "exist outside of God."[16] He proceeds by pointing out:

> You only need to remember the death of Christ to enter into . . . humility, because the essential message of the Cross is the power of pure love, a power that arises from total selflessness. The crucifix is there to remind us of our call to leave egoism behind and to understand otherness: to understand the power of true love.[17]

What does this tell about the fact that we sometimes have to drag ourselves to our meditation mats? Or that a certain unrest comes of us if we manage to get on it? Of course, part of the problem is that we often feel we are too busy—with our family, our job, the voluntary work we do. This, of course, is not without truth, although it remains worthwhile to continually ask ourselves how much of what we are doing is *really* necessary. What is the result of our choices that could be made differently and what is inevitably part of our present condition of life and calling?

However, I believe that our difficulties to start and keep on meditating might also originate from a deeper source. Doesn't it also relate to the fact that we don't really feel the need to root ourselves in the divine reality, because deep down we think we can deal with life on our own terms? This outlook may even give us a sense of power, of independence.

Yet are we not in fact saying the same as Jon Kabat-Zinn here? Are we not arguing now that we need to build a strong relationship with God for the moment our individual power might turn out to be insufficient? Not really, since an implication of Kabat-Zinn's phrase seems to be that in normal circumstances we *can* in fact do without a parachute. On the other hand, what has been said so far on the *theological context* of meditation is that while we are surely able to get

our groceries or celebrate our holidays without having integrated some kind of self-emptying practice in our daily lives,
we should perhaps admit we are living an ultimately superfi-
cial—in some important sense of the term *unreal*—life, since
the foundation and goal of life, its ultimate reality, is a God
inviting us into God's life.

Is living an unreal life necessarily bad? Well, apart from
the fact that living a half-life deprives us from a chance of
authenticity, of living according to reality, it also bears in it
a deadly risk for others and the planet. The pattern of thinking that lays behind it lures us in an isolated, self-sufficient,
inattentive, and, in the end, possessive condition of being. We
fail to integrate the sense of gift in our basic attitude to life.
That this condition is dangerous for others is illustrated by
our silent acceptance of the working conditions of those making our clothes in the sweatshop in Bangladesh or the daily
worsening ecological condition of our planet.

Main understands our inclination to live on our own
terms as an overtly present ego. This dominant ego impulse
is deeply rooted in the human person. Even when we have
managed to integrate a routine of twice-daily meditation,
or a similar practice, in our lives, we cannot say we have
definitely conquered the ego perspective on reality. We might
start feeling very satisfied about all the saintliness we show to
the world. Moreover, commitment remains important during our periods of meditation. Main emphasizes that it is
of great importance to keep saying the prayer word for the
whole time of the meditation. We should only consciously
stop when we feel like it might lead us into an ego-soothing
wellness spirituality in which the enjoyment of the peace we
have finally found in our busy lives becomes central. And it's
not only thoughts and images, which by necessity spring from

an egocentric viewpoint on reality—for they are always *my* thoughts, *my* images—that need to be left behind as an exercise in self-transcendence. Even our supposed conceptless and imageless silent state needs to be handed over as soon as we become aware of it.

Celebration through Growth

At the beginning of this chapter, I emphasized that the constitution of pure prayer is founded on a celebratory feast. In discussing the frequent elements of resistance to prayer, has this festive dimension of prayer once again been lost here? It depends on how you look at it. I have argued that we often feel distant from a sense of celebration when we are praying. It can feel like we are being dragged into the kingdom "kicking and screaming."[18] It seems an undeniable fact of our condition that all of us, to a greater or lesser degree, feel some resistance against the absoluteness of God's love. This situation requires a good deal of determinacy and sometimes struggle to overcome.

Yet, in the end, our condition is not one of an infinite, tragical fight but one of hope: "The loss of self . . . the erosion and the shedding of long familiar illusions require those qualities which have so important a place in St Paul's teaching: boldness, courage, faith, commitment, and perseverance. . . . These are not home-grown qualities, they are given to us by love, gifts from the Spirit to lead us to God, to deeper love."[19] Thus if and when we show the smallest willingness to open our lives to the process of divinization, of sharing in the feast of God's love, the Spirit of the crucified *but* resurrected Christ will carry us further.

Discipline has a close connection with the word *disciple*. Having (a) discipline shows a willingness, a determinacy to learn, to grow. Not in the sense of collecting ever more knowledge, more divine insights, which at will can be neatly phrased into propositions. Although this process implies a good deal of unlearning[20] egotistical habits, Main—and I with him—believes that ultimately it is an infinite process of growing into deeper love, a growth enabled by the gracious unification of our minds with the mind of Jesus.

Is this perspective not just as abstract as the future stressful disasters we, according to certain strands in mindfulness, should prepare ourselves for? Well, faith, as Paul stresses in Romans 1:17, remains important from the beginning till the end of our journey on earth. Yet, in my personal experience, the growth engendered by meditation it not abstract. Slowly, very slowly, a sense of the intimacy of God's presence in my life grows. In one moment, not long ago, I suddenly realized I didn't necessarily need to close my eyes anymore during the moments of collective prayer during a Eucharist celebration. It occurred to me, on an experiential level, that everything around me—the objects, the people, the sounds of the organ, the songs, the light shining from one of the windows through the burning incense—is one great mysterious prayer in which God lives, is present very close to me.

Another reason for a festive spirit is that I gradually have become aware of how beautifully different the people are who come to meditation groups to meditate together. Along with people who in terms of "the world" would be conceived as successful, there are beautiful creatures who join these groups who are perhaps less fortunate according to the worldly standards. What is more, the very successful types often become soft and leave behind the fears that would otherwise perhaps prevent them from sharing some of their vulnerabilities—perhaps the fear of losing precisely those things that support their success. Aren't these divine miracles? "Because of this, prayer is the great school of community,"[21] as Main often emphasizes, and a very beautiful, divine community has become reality in front of my eyes.

Obviously I hope to become more loving, less easily annoyed by other people's thoughts or habits, although this type of growth—the most important one—is not for me to judge. When they see how I can react to neighbors who in my view are a bit too noisy, some people doubt the effect it has on me. Thank God I can always reply that without meditation everything would probably have been even worse.

Celebrating the Discipline of Christian Meditation in a Secular Age

Often when I teach meditation explicitly from the theological perspective that has been the focus of this chapter, a sense of estrangement comes over me. My festive mood sometimes even gets stifled by my awareness of the spiritual condition in which I am living. I become aware of the *strangeness* of recognizing in the crucified and tortured body of Jesus the ultimate expression of the Divine and even more so of my strong conviction that this faith is and remains extremely relevant for the practice of prayer, of meditation as I understand it. It is a strangeness that was felt by the Romans: they saw it as a reason for mockery as becomes clear from the ancient caricature of the crucified donkey. However, the sense of strangeness of this faith has increased by the fact that while in the times of the Romans, conceiving the transcendent as a dimension of reality was the general outlook. Right now, as Charles Taylor famously has argued in his *A Secular Age*, religious faith is just one option among many. It is an outlook, Taylor points out, that furthermore finds itself within a framework, an implicit set of tentative beliefs, which many interpret as completely closed toward the Transcendent. Hence "the immanent frame."[22]

Taylor explains that this framework imagines the human person as closed to spirits, demons, and other external causal powers, in short as "a buffered self," as engaged in practices of self-discipline and as a personally responsible individual who is part of an impersonal moral order instead of embedded in a divinely ordered and sustained society. Moreover, the cosmos is seen as governed by exceptionless and natural laws. Often this way of imagining the human person and society is presented by the deniers of transcendence as a natural result of a process of both scientific discovery and personal liberation, a process of freeing oneself from the superstitious, extremist, ordinary-life despising and violent tendencies of religion.

It seems undeniable that certain aspects of the medieval understanding of the cosmos couldn't survive critical reason as represented by natural science. It is also true that religion has often been defending an anti-bodily spirituality and more than once has been entangled with categorical and brute violence. Taylor, however, points at a tension between those denying a transcendent reality that is worth pondering. He points at the fact that those proposing that the ordinary life of family, work, and consuming is the ideal life, meet within their own nonreligious camp a resistance from philosophers who think that the aspiration of human beings in this way is censored or mutilated. They propose a life that is more exciting, more mysterious, than the docile life humanists propose. Popular expressions of this feeling can be seen in movies such as *Fight Club* or in the gangs of violent hooligans looking for a thrill. Isn't this an indication that the nonreligious, humanist condition in the end is less stable, less fulfilling than some would like to have it?

To me, this tension, including its violent dimensions, is an indication of the reasonableness, or at least of the not-unreasonableness, of the religious option as presented in Christian mystical theology. Can there be a more exciting picture of life than that of an infinite expansion into the exuberant, essentially nonviolent life of the Trinity?

Perhaps the secret pull of such a life-form is the reason why one of my coolest pupils, Timothy, age fourteen, who is very popular with his classmates yet not always easy for his teachers, came to tell me the other day that after my introduction on meditation he had tried it on his own in his bedroom. Maybe this is also the reason why he, half seriously, half jokingly, keeps on giving me updates on his latest insights and asks me what he should read to find inspiration "to live" more truly "in the here and now."

Timothy's views on meditation as I understand them are still far from those presented above. It goes without saying that one shouldn't throw the full picture of the Christian theological context of meditation in his face immediately. I think both the spiritual condition of the secular age we inhabit in general and the strangeness of the Christian faith in particular make advisable an approach to teaching meditation that takes its inspiration from Jesus's way of dealing with his disillusioned pupils on the road to Emmaus (Lk 24:13–35). This implies that we walk with (potential) meditators from the point in life where they *are*, and not from the point one would like them to be.

Having said this, I also believe that maintaining a close connection with the Christian mystical-*theological* tradition when we teach meditation is important for two reasons. It will enable us to remain faithful to the fact that the One accompanying us in the Spirit into the Divine is the One crucified by the hands of humanity, and the self-knowledge and reflection this very fact asks for. And it will hopefully enable us to be a serious sparring partner of those who are not satisfied with the first feeling of "wow" after having been introduced to meditation and need further encouragement and motivation to remain faithful to the discipline of meditation.[23]

Notes

1. Cf. John Main, *Word Into Silence,* ed. Laurence Freeman (Norwich, UK: Canterbury Press, 2006), 13.

2. Charles Taylor, *A Secular Age* (Cambridge, MA: Belknap Press, 2007).

3. Taylor, *Secular Age,* 539–93.

4. For further details of Main's life, see, for instance, Neil McKenty, *In the Stillness Dancing: The Life of Father John Main* (New York: Crossroad, 1987).

5. Much of what follows is based on Main's account of it as he renders it in *Christian Meditation: The Gethsemani Talks* (London: Medio Media, 1999).

6. See, for instance, Thomas Keating, *Intimacy with God: An Introduction to Centering Prayer* (New York: Crossroad, 2013), xvii.

7. Main also mentions similarities between the practice of the Jesus Prayer as developed early in the spiritual tradition of the Eastern Orthodox Church or the practice of the twentieth-century spiritual author Simone Weil. The latter recommends that slow and attentive praying of the Our Father as a practice to simplify and center our mind upon the Divine. Cf. Main, *Community of Love* (New York: Continuum, 1999), 102–7.

8. John Cassian, "The Conferences," trans. and notes Edgar C. S. Gibson, in *A Select Library of Nicene and Post-Nicene Fathers of the Christian*

Church, 2nd ser., vol. 2, ed. Philip Schaff and Henry Wace (Buffalo, NY: Christian Literature Publishing, 1894), 330.

9. Main, *Christian Meditation,* 22.

10. Main, *Word Into Silence,* 43.

11. Main, *Word Into Silence,* 18–19.

12. John Main, *Moment of Christ: The Path of Meditation* (New York: Continuum, 2005), 43.

13. Mark A. McIntosh, *Mystical Theology* (Oxford: Blackwell, 1998), 122.

14. McIntosh, *Mystical Theology,* 123. Italics are mine.

15. John Main, *The Present Christ* (New York: Crossroad, 1986), 116. Italics are mine. See also Main, *Community of Love,* 111.

16. John Main, *The Heart of Creation: Meditation—a Way of Setting God Free in the World* (Norwich, UK: Canterbury Press, 2007), 23.

17. John Main, *The Way of Unknowing: Expanding Spiritual Horizons through Meditation* (Eugene, OR: Wipf and Stock, 2004), 125.

18. John Main, *Door to Silence: An Anthology for Christian Meditation* (Norwich, UK: Canterbury Press, 2006), 74.

19. Main, *Word Into Silence,* 27.

20. Main, *Moment of Christ,* 53.

21. Main, *Word Into Silence,* 72.

22. My portrayal of Taylor's concept of the immanent frame in this section is based on Taylor, *Secular Age,* 539–93.

23. Charles Taylor, *Varieties of Religion Today: William James Revisited* (Cambridge, MA: Harvard University Press, 2003), 116.

The Power of
Contemplative Symbols

JESSICA M. SMITH

Those of us who gathered for the New Contemplative Exchange at Snowmass had diverse backgrounds and experiences. We came from four different strands of contemplative communities, different countries, and different traditions (Protestant, Anglican, and Catholic); some of us were lay and some clergy or religious. Some of us were married, others single.

Our time together revealed that we have different understandings of the goals and methods of contemplative practice. Some understand a practitioner's ultimate aim to be an apophatic union with God; in this school of thought, in the midst of repeating a word in meditation, there can be a moment of union with God in which the word eventually falls away. Others hold steadfast to the importance of the sacred word and that any other emotion, thought, or experience—no matter how euphoric or illuminating—is still only the self or ego coming to expression. Still others of us are more focused on a broad array of ways to live contemplatively understanding the uniqueness of each person. This respect for the *imago dei* in each person encourages individuals to find their particular way on the path of contemplation rather than ascribing to a single, uniform, and universal method of contemplative practice.

Among these differences, however, some basic configurations were similar. The simple practice of sitting in silence in a circle was implicitly familiar to members of the contemplative exchange right as we met. On the first night, we gathered in a beautiful meeting space at St. Benedict's Monastery. Without much instruction, each of us walked into the soft-carpeted room and found a *zafu* or a chair before coming to the circle. Some sat in lotus position with their eyes closed. Others sat in chairs, eyes open. Nods of recognition were offered across the room. We settled into silence. A *kesu* (iron gong) sat on the floor with its striker beside it. One person picked up the striker and tapped on the kesu.[1] Without a word, the whole group understood this was the bell calling us to silence. After the period of silence, the kesu was struck once more. Some bowed, others stretched their arms, and others sat with a soft gaze.

Why did we all come together without instruction, and respond the way we did to the bell? Why did this all seem so familiar and yet we had never gathered together before? The ubiquity of certain symbols in contemporary Christian contemplative practice (e.g. the circle, the bell) express across different schools of practice and thought deep theological convictions about the nature of divine reality.

In my own personal practice, I have a small table that sits beside a chair. On the table, are two main items: a candle and a bell. The candle is small and unobtrusive. The bell sits on a little pillow with its striker resting beside it. Each time I sit, I set the timer on my phone, light the candle, strike the bell, and close my eyes. I repeat a sacred word, returning to it when I grow distracted. When the timer goes off, I open my eyes, strike the bell, and blow out the candle. I didn't pick the bell and the candle out of my spontaneous impulses; rather, the practice called for the symbols.

As I've reflected a bit more on the symbolic power of the bell and the lit candle, I've realized that they express deep commitments common in contemplative Christian practice. The bell and the candle awaken ideas of depth, spaciousness, stillness, attunement, and luminosity—all deep commitments in contemplative Christian practice. When I strike the kesu or light the candle—in a circle with others, or alone—there is a resonant meaning in the symbols for contemplative practice.

In the following meditation, I will first say a bit more about what I mean by *symbol*. Then I will consider the work of the bell and the flame symbolically. Finally, I will consider how the ideal nature of symbols can help us return to contemplative commitments with a fresh understanding of both the imperfections of human practice and the inherent mysteries of contemplation.

A Word about Symbols

Symbols such as bells, candles, the cross, and the eucharistic cup and bread are rooted in power, unwavering in their expression of ultimate reality.[2] To me, they stand and express power similar to that of a giant old tree standing in the middle of a field, rarely shaken by what is around it while offering beauty, shelter, and strength to the world. Occasionally, I stand at my apartment window gazing at a majestic oak tree that stands a good seven stories tall outside my building. One afternoon, a giant thunderstorm was barreling through the mid-Atlantic. I marveled at how the giant tree with full leaves waved its branches with each gust of wind, and burst of rain and thunder. Yet, when the storm passed, the tree stood still, unmoved. It was as if the storm had never shaken it.

Symbols such as the bell and candle are similar. They express their power and open connection to the Divine, resilient yet responsive to the elements surrounding them.

Symbols always exceed what we say about them.[3] They touch us in ways that are beyond any single description precisely because they are connected to that which is of ultimate concern, of the infinite and transcendent reality. They are simple and compact, and they express a constellation of related and interconnected meanings all at once. As the philosopher Paul Ricoeur notes, symbols are more powerful than a single description yet precisely more mysterious and opaque because of their constitution. This is both their power and their difficulty.

Contemplative practice is especially attuned to the power of symbols and expresses the eternal and the ultimate in fresh, *meaning-full* ways. Symbols are literally full of meaning. They turn us away from our immediate preoccupations and toward the real, and the truly manifest.

The Kesu: A Symbol of Depth, Spaciousness, Stillness, Attunement

How good it is to center down!
To sit quietly and see one's self pass by!
The streets of our minds seethe with endless traffic;
Our spirits resound with clashings, with noisy silences
. . . .
As we listen, floating up through all the jangling echoes of our turbulence, there is a sound of another kind—
A deeper note which only the stillness of the heart makes clear.[4]

HOWARD THURMAN

The kesu, or the singing bowl, differs from the bells traditionally rung in Western Christianity such as church bells, altar bells, or sacring bells. First, the kesu makes sound differently. A church bell hangs upside down with a clapper inside the bell. When the bell moves and sways, the clapper hits the interior of the bell to make its sound. The kesu, on the other hand, is an open bowl-shaped object. The sound of the kesu comes from a striker hitting its rim, but its interior is empty. The kesu resonates with contemplative practice because it helps express the contemplative commitment to the deep, spacious interior, or what Tilden Edwards calls the spiritual heart.

The bell's empty interior reminds us to find our way toward a deeper way of being—where the interior is still and empty. For some contemplatives, this movement toward emptiness comes from the work of self-emptying. Perhaps there are ways in which one must let go or empty one's self from preoccupations or worries that arise from what the spiritual director Lerita Coleman Brown calls "ego chatter." The ego can become so formidable and prominent that the self begins to believe that its personal perceptions are both the center of reality and the ultimate in their constitution. There is a word of caution, however. The ego isn't necessarily a negative thing. The theologian Wendy Farley notes that an "egological" sensibility[5] is important for regulating pain, hunger, and pleasure. Without this sensibility, the human being could not live in the everyday. However, as Farley relates, the egological structure tends to become egocentric. Such egocentrism may necessitate ways to redirect attention away from the ego's preoccupations and worries.

In addition to the egocentric tendencies in the self, Tilden Edwards articulates the "thinking mind" is another dominant place out of which we live. It is an important part of the human life to discern and categorize what we see. Labeling, categorizing, and naming objects in the world enables us to communicate with others and navigate through the world. However, to have a more immediate, direct, and intuitive awareness of divine presence is too "obscure" for the thinking mind. As Edwards writes, "In a sense, the thinking mind cannot be fully at home spiritually, since its very cognitive structure keeps it as an outside observer of direct spiritual awareness."[6] In other words, the structure of the way we categorize and know things as objects cannot adequately be directly and immediately present to what is.

Regardless of their dominance in any particular time or situation, Edwards helpfully names that there is a third space out of which we might live. This is the spiritual heart. Rather than a rejection of the ego self, it is a movement in the self from the ego self to a deeper, spacious, welcoming place. It is a place where we connect to the eternal and out of which we more directly and intuitively know prior to what we label or conceptualize the world. It is a knowing beyond and behind whatever conscious thought or image we may attach to it. Edwards argues that we can be invited to "lean back" into a deeper reality within us. There, he says, is a spaciousness and a home, where we might live out of what he terms "contemplative awareness."

This work of decentering the ego and the thinking mind is not easy. Over the course of the day, my thoughts and emotions, worries and fears begin to take up space in me. My mind whirs with analysis and explanation for why that person said something a few days ago that made me mad, or remembers a past love who keeps sticking to my heart, or replays habits I cannot shake, or berates me for that extra glass of wine I drank last night. Too often I am like a blocked bell. Even when I take a breath and close my eyes, to begin my practice I am often flooded with thoughts and emotions whirring along.

However, after a bit of time in silence, it's like I'm quieting my interior in order to drop into this heart-space. The phenomenal thing about this deeper interior is that, like the interior of the bell, there is a spaciousness in the interior depth beneath. With this spaciousness comes freedom to live and move out of the heart. The interior depth of the bell reminds me of the spacious beauty of the spiritual heart, uncluttered and connected to the eternal.

Second, the practitioner can take inspiration from the bell on the gift of stillness. Before the bell rings out from being struck on its rim, it sits very still. Altar bells typically hang with a handle, with the bells dangling below. Their sound comes from the bell moving back and forth. A kesu, on the other hand, sits still on a cushion and produces sound as a striker approaches its rim. When struck, the bell rings out with a commanding vibration. Its waves of sound ripple outward unfettered.

Stillness enables the vibrations to resound outward. Similarly, as Howard Thurman describes in his poem on centering down, there is a "stillness of the heart." It is out of this stillness of the heart that a clear "deeper note" floats to the surface. This note is of a different tone, a different resonance from that which we hear in particular words, thoughts, or feelings. It is an attunement of the heart that is clearer and more beautiful than all the "jangling echoes" of our cluttered minds and egos. Stillness, as Lerita Coleman Brown describes, allows us to listen to the Spirit. If we remain with our ego chatter, as she puts it, then we cannot hear anything deeper.[7] To be still allows us to hear not just with our minds but with our whole selves what the Spirit may be offering or inviting.

There is also a clarity with being still. When a stream flows quickly over rocks and causes rough waters, we cannot see clearly beneath the surface of the stream. Still waters grant us an ability to see into its depths. If we can still ourselves enough, we can receive what is invited by the Source of all flowing up within us. We can have a better sense of who we are and what lies beneath the surface of our thoughts and feelings;

The bell's beauty and power arise when it is struck and its tone resonates from its center outward. Like the bell with its hollow core, the contemplative can participate in the divine rippling out from its core. In the stillness of the spiritual heart, the vibrations of love resonate outward the vibration attuned to the Divine. In contemplative practice, divine and human activity are understood to be attuned to one·another. God's love is not somehow outside or beyond us, but among, between, and within us.

In a recent reflection by Richard Rohr titled "A Tuning Fork," he writes,

> Prayer is connecting with God/Ultimate Reality. It is not an attempt to change God's mind about us or about events. . . . Prayer is primarily about changing our own mind so that things like infinity, mystery, and forgiveness can resound within us. The small mind cannot see great things because the two are on different frequencies or channels. We must match our resonance to Love's. Like knows like.[8]

Our whole being can be a vessel attuned to God's love rippling out throughout the world around us. To resonate with the Divine is a way of communing with God, delighting and finding refreshment in that spaciousness of the spiritual heart.

The Flame: Luminosity, Illumination, Vitality

> Kindle Thy light within me, O God, that Thy glow
> may be spread over all of my life; yea indeed, that Thy
> glow may be spread over all my life. More and more,
> may Thy light give radiance to my flickering candle,
> fresh vigor to my struggling intent, and renewal to my
> flagging spirit. Without Thy light within me, I must
> spend my year fumbling in my darkness.[9]

The image of light has long been a symbol of experiencing a direct encounter with the Divine that illuminates our
lives. The twentieth-century Christian mystic Evelyn Underhill notes that much of this illuminative imagery is seen in the
prologue to the Gospel of John.[10] The Nicene Creed names
God as being "light of light, True God from true God." God
is the unbegotten one whose being emanates love and life
eternally without cause or succession.

With this long stream of light imagery, it is no wonder it continues to be a deep and powerful symbol of mysticism. Underhill
helpfully identifies three characteristics of illumination in the
mystical path. First, illumination expresses the joyous awareness of the Divine in relation to the self. Second, the illuminative moment also can cause a "clarity of vision" with respect to
the everyday world around us.[11] She writes, "The self perceives
an added significance and reality in all natural things."[12] Third,
the self may experience visions, inspirational writing, or audi-
tory experiences that are attributed to the Divine. Underhill is
careful to note there is intense debate around this final characteristic. She leaves visions and voices open to question, but
recognizes that for many they bring wisdom and calm.

Lighting a candle reminds us of the inner light within
ourselves. We are reminded of our own inner light and the

presence of God. Wendy Farley refers to this intimate relationship between our interior spirits and the divine light as the luminosity of our being. For her, this luminosity reflects the spark or aspect of the Divine that lives within each of us:

> Deeper than the distortions of our lives is a beauty and luminosity . . . this luminosity is known by many names: the image of God, Buddha mind, Atman is Brahman, or, in Lincoln's words, "the angels of our better nature."[13]

St. Augustine beautifully writes about the ways he encounters such illumination:

> With you as my guide I entered into my innermost citadel, and was given power to do so because you had become my helper (Ps. 29:11). I entered and my soul's eye, such as it was, saw above that same eye of my soul the immutable light higher than my mind.[14]

When we enter into the inner most parts of ourselves, we might be guided to this light within that is part of the divine light; the inner luminosity of our being grows brighter as we connect with the divine eternal.

Equally significant is that this inner experience of illumination can, in the words of Underhill, "expand" our awareness of the divine presence in the world. This dimension of illumination is best described, she writes, as "an enhanced mental lucidity—an abnormal sharpening of the senses—whereby an ineffable radiance, a beauty and a reality never before suspected, are perceived by a sort of clairvoyance shining in the meanest things."[15] In other words, illumination does not only bring greater awareness of God's presence and connection to God within one's self but also helps shed light and therefore greater awareness on the infinite beauty of the divine reality radiating through even the most mundane of encounters.

Such an illumination is invigorating; it is life giving. This encounter can give, as Thurman notes, "fresh vigor" and "renewal" to one's spirit. This renewal and vitality relate to who God is. Certainly light is vital for life. Plants need its energy to grow and live; the gravitational pull of the sun keeps Earth in orbit. Similarly, the Divine is the source of life. As Thurman writes, its "glow may be spread over all my life." In other words, the experience of illumination is both a connection inward to the spark of the Divine within and can help us see more deeply what matters in the way we move and live in the world. It spreads over one's whole life. As Thurman writes, without the gift of illumination, we are left "stumbling in the darkness." Just as one stumbles in a dark room without a candle or a flashlight, when we are unable to be connected to the Divine, we cannot find our way very well.

In the summer of 2017, the week before the New Contemplative Exchange at Snowmass, I was attending a World Community of Christian Meditation conference in Houston, Texas, with a group of about 150 meditators from around the world. At the same time, on Saturday, August 12, 2017, a white supremacy rally was held at Emancipation Park, in Charlottesville, Virginia, sparked by debate over a Robert E. Lee statue that stands in that town—my hometown. Counter rallies and members of the community also came out, and consequent agitation and violence erupted. That day, a young man ran his car into a crowd of counterprotesters, killing one young woman, Heather Heyer. My sister's family and my parents stayed home that afternoon listening to helicopters overhead. I could only watch from afar as my hometown was being magnified by the media for a horrid drama unfolding.

Back in Houston, I was fortunate to be staying near the world-renowned Rothko Chapel. Rothko Chapel is an octagonal building that serves as an interfaith chapel and stands for human rights, activism, and the arts. The abstract expressionist painter Mark Rothko designed the space and the fourteen giant canvases displayed there. The tall dark canvases stand against a stark white background. Sunlight passes across the space through a window at the top of the octagonal shape. While light can enter, it is indirectly experienced. One cannot look up and see the sky above because there is an octagonal shape hanging from the ceiling. This allows for the light to pour over and out to the edges of the chapel space but does not allow the viewer to see directly up into the sky. Simple, dark wooden benches sit in the middle of the space, with zafus positioned beside them. Brick stones reminiscent of big city sidewalks line the floor. The previous day, Fr. Laurence Freeman had led us in a reflection in the chapel and noted that the best way to view each piece of art was by to stand eighteen inches from the canvas.

So in my state of unease, and feeling helpless to be there for my hometown, I walked dazed toward the chapel and was drawn to one of the canvases. I could feel myself needing to be in Rothko Chapel; I needed to stand in the dark and be refreshed by its quiet and its presence. I stood about eighteen inches from the canvas and stared as motionless as I could at the darkness.

As I stood there, the sounds from emergency room beds filled with people in pain and bloodied flashed in my head. The cries of many in Charlottesville and then still the cries of so many emerged. I felt the pain flowing into the canvas and also expressed by it. After some time, I slowly craned my neck upward and saw a soft light peer through from above.

I could not see the light's origins, but as I followed the light back to the canvas, I realized that the canvas shimmered, and even flecks of silver flashed in places. Through the illumination from the light above I was able to see anew and experience both darkness and light in a new way. Just as I could not control the light appearing so strongly across the canvas, I could not control its stay. Just as it had gently passed over the canvas, so too did it gently fade.

I hold my encounter in Rothko Chapel very close to my heart. Of course, it did not instantly resolve the injustices of racism and white supremacy around the world. I didn't hear any clear instruction from the Divine. But it did give me a sense of inner knowing about the ineffable, mysterious love of God. It helped my thinking mind and my ego self settle back into the heart-space when the world was ringing with pain. The streaks of silver against the black canvas gave me hope about the shining souls that are working every day to bring healing in a wounded world.

Through illumination we can be refreshed and reinvigorated. We may find hope and a way to move in the world in the midst of heartbreak and pain. We may find a way to allow the light within us to burn brightly through our renewed connection with the Divine.

Symbols: Their Dangers and Their Gift for Practice

The bell and the flame are a gift and an inspiration. They conjure up thoughts of stillness, depth, spaciousness, and luminosity. They remind me of my commitments to contemplative practice. But I would feel untrue if I left this meditation extolling the virtues of symbols without also offering a caution in general.

First, I think that symbols manifest commitments and ideals, but they in themselves are not human beings. They may hold the power to bring to mind important aspects of contemplative living. But, at the same time, I have found that anything can become an impediment to contemplative awareness. Even the symbols and the practices themselves can become those impediments.

Kim Boykin remarks in her book on practicing Zen that there was a period of time when she was wrestling with her practice, and she realized that she was still trying to control the practice itself. As she describes, "I had been trying to use my spiritual practice to get what I wanted, when spiritual practice is actually about being with reality as it is."[16] In other words, the practice was ego-driven. She read Gerald May's classic *Will and Spirit* and it gave her a new vocabulary for the difference between willfully practicing (which ends in struggle) and the "willingness" of true contemplative practice. She goes on to remark that even after she realized this insight, she still found herself trying to "practice willingness willfully."[17] Even when she thought she could show up to practice in a new way, she found herself still thinking thoughts about how returning to her practice "would be *good for me*. That is, I would immediately fall back into making my Zen practice an instrument of my will."[18] I identify with Kim's account. At times, I find myself watching myself meditating and think to myself, "Aren't I doing so well, because I'm sitting here trying to connect with God? I'm such a good person." The practice becomes about my self-image. Upon realizing this inner reality, I typically beat myself up further for my misstep, only putting me ever deeper into a quagmire. This is the truth.

To get me out of my own inner critic, sometimes it takes another member of my community to bring me back to a place of forgiveness and belonging. It may take hearing someone I trust pray with me to hear my own fears and hurts, to spend time in the silence, and to offer a prayer of the heart out loud for me. Or sometimes I need to go run outside and look at the trees. Sometimes it takes singing "Everybody's Got a Right to Live" on the streets of Washington DC with the Poor People's Campaign. Whatever it is, sometimes I have to get outside myself in order to return to my practice without the need to control or determine the outcome.

When I come to my practice willingly and without force, I appreciate the symbolism of the candle and the flame together, because they hold mystery and paradox together. When I see the candle lit beside the bell, it reminds me that contemplative awareness and the spiritual heart are like the vital flame of a candle *and* an empty, open space. There is illumination and spacious stillness; it is the hope and warmth of being alive, and it is my soul resonating and being attuned to God. These are expressions of the paradox of contemplative awareness. Light and dark, depth and illumination, stillness and vitality. The symbols of flame and bell together and the symbolic tension they produce in their juxtaposition keeps me from staying too close to any single expression. They remind me that I cannot grasp or comprehend or control the Divine. They invite me to practice with them together or between them, to allow their power that is connected to the eternal inspire and awaken that same connection within me.

Returning in my mind to the circle in a meeting room of St. Benedict's Monastery, I am all the more aware of the gift of symbols. They are unifying even in the midst of diverse understandings of practice. However we understand the practice, we also light candles and ring bells. We sit on zafus and chairs and close our eyes. We pray for the world in the still spacious heart, and we burn bright and luminous in the divine love.

Notes

1. The introduction of *kesus* and *zafus* reflects the innovation in contemplative Christian prayer through Christian encounters with Buddhist tradition in the last half of the twentieth century. As Louis Komjathy notes, much of the rise of meditation practice in the second half of the twentieth century corresponds with an influx of Asian immigrants to the United States after the new immigration law in 1965. A rise in Asian immigrants led to greater access to teachers as well as, Komjathy writes, "increasing numbers of religious communities associated with them and their spiritual successors, and to greater access to Asian meditation schools, especially those associated with Buddhism and Hinduism" (23). He is quick to note that simultaneous to this new wave of meditation teachers and communities was a shift in Catholicism with the Second Vatican Council as well as greater attention to ecumenism and interreligious dialogue. Thus for many contemporary Christians, increased exposure to meditative practices from Asia brought new insights into practicing contemplation. Along with new practices of zazen, yoga, and koan meditation, this cross-pollination between Christian and Buddhist practice also inspired creative integration of zafus, bells, and gongs such as the kesu from these traditions into Christian contemplative spaces.

2. Thanks to Fr. Laurence Freeman for awakening in me the beauty and power of symbols and the thought of the philosopher Paul Ricoeur through his talks at the World Community of Christian Meditation conference, Houston, Texas.

3. See Paul Ricoeur, *Interpretation Theory: Discourse and the Surplus of Meaning* (Fort Worth: Texas Christian University Press, 1976).

4. Howard Thurman, "How Good to Center Down!" *Meditations of the Heart* (Boston: Beacon Press, 1999) 28–29. Also, thanks to Lerita

Coleman-Brown for bringing this particular meditation to my awareness at a retreat on Howard Thurman.

5. Wendy Farley, *The Wounding and Healing of Desire* (Louisville, KY: Westminster John Knox Press, 2005), 32–33.

6. Tilden Edwards, *Embracing the Call to Spiritual Depth: Gifts for Contemplative Living* (Mahwah, NJ: Paulist Press, 2010), 11–12.

7. Lerita Colman Brown, "Lerita Coleman Brown, PhD: Howard Thurman and the Inner Authority of Silence," EncounteringSilence.com, February 7, 2018, http://encounteringsilence.com/lerita-coleman-brown -phd-howard-thurman-and-the-inner-authority-of-silence.

8. Richard Rohr, "A Tuning Fork," Center for Action and Contemplation, June 30, 2017, https://cac.org/a-tuning-fork-2017-06-30.

9. Howard Thurman, *Meditations of the Heart* (Boston: Beacon Press, 1981), 159–60.

10. Evelyn Underhill, *Mysticism* (Mineola, NY: Dover Publications, 2002), 323.

11. Underhill, *Mysticism*, 164.

12. Underhill, *Mysticism*, 164.

13. Farley, *Wounding and Healing of Desire*, 20.

14. Augustine, *Confessions*, trans. Henry Chadwick (Oxford: Oxford University Press, 1998), 7.10. Thanks to Evelyn Underhill's notation of this passage in *Mysticism*.

15. Underhill, *Mysticism*, 174.

16. Kim Boykin, *Zen for Christians: A Beginner's Guide* (San Francisco: Jossey-Bass, 2003), 34.

17. Boykin, *Zen for Christians*, 34.

18. Boykin, *Zen for Christians*, 34.

TRANSFORMATION IN COMMUNITY

A Primary Concern for Oneness

Contemplation and Leadership in Congregations

STUART HIGGINBOTHAM

> *Our whole business in this life*
> *is to restore to health the eye of the heart*
> *whereby God may be seen.*[1]
>
> —St. Augustine

> *The desperate need today is not for a greater number*
> *of intelligent people,*
> *or gifted people, but for deep people.*[2]
>
> —Richard J. Foster

Gathering at St. Benedict's Monastery in Snowmass, Colorado, in August 2017 was an extraordinary opportunity for deep reflection and exploration. I found myself surrounded by colleagues from around the world whose diverse vocations exemplified the promise of the Spirit to weave Christ's reconciling message into all lives. The diverse charisms and experiences made my heart swell, and I yearned to translate the experience into my own life as a husband, father, and parish priest.

In this chapter I will build on those shared conversations in Snowmass and explore the intersection of three pivotal areas: the dynamics of a contemplative grounding, the complexities of congregational development, and the challenges of pastoral leadership. This particular junction is the space in which my own vocation continues to be nurtured and honed.

The Dynamics of a Contemplative Grounding

Four years ago, when I began my cure at Grace Episcopal Church, I shared a lunch conversation with a key parish leader. "We're wondering when you're going to be more aggressive," he told me over fried green beans. As he spoke, I was vividly aware that I was embarking on a journey for which I felt ill-equipped. At that point, I had only been a priest some six years, and I found myself the rector of a parish and preschool of over twelve hundred people. Self-doubt was my constant companion. She joined me for every conversation I shared with the experienced lay leaders of the parish.

For over a year I had shared in the discernment process with Grace Church. I tried to listen deeply to what they were saying, and I tried to listen even more deeply to what the Spirit was saying between us within the conversations we shared. My clergy profile was filled with my own reflections and questions of what leadership within a community looked like. I had been as honest as possible about my own deep desire for a leadership style that was contemplatively oriented—marked by prayer, discernment, and dialogue rather than by the seemingly ubiquitous corporate management style.

My ongoing experiences with the Shalem Institute for Spiritual Formation had shown me that my own yearning for a different way of pastoral leadership was a hope shared by many. I described to both the search committee and the vestry my own priority to maintain my practice of prayer as the grounding of my parish leadership. I knew the demands on my time would be high, with attention going toward budget details, stewardship, program development, staff coordination, community relationships, worship planning, newcomer orientation, pastoral care, outreach, and the spiritual health of all the souls entrusted to my care. A lot was expected of me, to be sure. In order to "do this" well, I had to maintain my own practice of prayer and silence. It was not an option if my heart was to sustain the pace and pressure.

As well as being the ground of my own personal practice, I was also curious if it was possible for an entire community to be grounded in practices of contemplative prayer to orient ourselves around discernment and dialogue, to trust and listen for the Spirit's guidance, and to risk exploring a posture of contemplative awareness and transformation. For the entire year of the search process we shared these conversations, and they kept inviting me back for further discussions. They were curious too.

When I knew I was one of the final three candidates, I met with my bishop and shared surprise and anticipation, in equal measure. I was excited, of course, that this potential space existed for me and my family, and I was quite surprised that the community seemed to be curious about the same things I was. The Spirit was very much at work, and I felt I could trust that. In the subsequent five years we have shared, I continue to be inspired by both the Spirit's guiding presence and the community's willingness to engage from the spiritual heart.

Given my own experience and the growth of our community, I am convinced that such a *contemplative reformation* is essential within the institutional church in light of the challenges we face. The Spirit has shown me what can happen when a group of people lean in to a space of attunement with the Spirit's movement. The staff, vestry, committee members, and parishioners have opened themselves to a personally risky, heart-centered space of shared ministry. Together we have already seen how fruit can be borne from holding a contemplative posture in our shared ministry, a willingness to be receptive to insight and guidance from the Spirit that is mindful of our tendency for egoic grasping. Our story has not been without struggle and frustration, yet the hope we have encountered leads us to trust all the more in the potential of a contemplative reformation.

When it comes to the mission of the church, the Episcopal Church offers a succinct statement in our catechism:

Q: "What is the mission of the Church?"

A: "The mission of the church is to restore all people to unity with God and each other in Christ."[3]

While this particular language is from *The Book of Common Prayer*, it speaks to a common understanding shared across denominational frameworks. Throughout the wider Christian community, we recognize the way we feel estranged from ourselves, from a deeper awareness of God's presence, and we yearn for salvation and wholeness.

The catechism in *The Book of Common Prayer* offers this powerful image of a desire for restoration which, by definition, speaks to a return to a previous state of being from which we have become estranged or removed. Given our shared lens of the contemplative tradition within Christianity, it behooves us at this point to reflect more deeply on this language of restoration to unity. What are we speaking of when we claim this restoration as foundational to the church's mission? Just what is being restored?

When we speak of unity and *oneness*, we are, of course, speaking of the nature of our union with God—and one another. One of the hallmarks of the contemplative tradition is that union with God is the basis of our identity.[4] We *are* united with God, God with us; however, we struggle with a lack of awareness of the true nature of things. We live and act as though God is distant from us when, in fact, God is the deep reality in which "we live and move and have our being" (Acts 17:28), as St. Paul describes to the Athenians. Put another way, it is our perception that is warped, and we come to believe that transcendence in terms of God's being and essence denotes a distance in God's location and proximity, a separation. As the twentieth-century spiritual teacher Eknath Easwaran succinctly says, "We see life not as it is but as we are."[5]

Indeed, our texts and tradition constantly remind us of the unitive ground of our existence, although we so often seem to look past this core reality. The Psalmist attests to this foundational oneness:

> You hem me in, behind and before,
> And lay your hand upon me.
> Such knowledge is too wonderful for me;
> It is so high that I cannot attain it.
> Where can I go from your spirit?
> Or where can I flee from your presence?
>
> (Ps 139:5–7)

As the theologian A. M. Allchin describes, the central affirmations about Jesus's life and ministry

speak about a meeting, a union of God with human-
kind that alters our understanding, our deepest experience of what it is to be human, which gives us a
new vision of the whole creation and alters the basic
substance of our living and dying.[6]

In terms of a contemplative understanding of our catechism, therefore, what is being restored is a greater awareness
of our unity with God and one another in Christ. The Roman
Catholic theologian Raimon Panikkar's words in particular
may be helpful as he reflects on how the nature of this union
is essential to our understanding of a life of faith:

At the basis of faith, therefore, is an experience of
union. I do not wish to be misunderstood. The word
"experience" is ambiguous and polysemic. In this
instance it is not a question of mere psychological
experience, but of an ontological "touch," so to speak.
It is an experience that transforms our entire being; we
have a feeling that we have been taken over by a stronger reality that penetrates and transforms us.[7]

In this way, we are called to orient ourselves toward this
deepest principle of our existence rather than persist in the
illusion of separateness that lends itself toward categorization
and an egoic grasping for power and control. In the teachings of the contemplative tradition—grounded as they are in
the scriptural experience of the unitive reorientation ushered
in by Jesus's life, death, and resurrection—we see the potential within such a shift in awareness. While our words fail to
grasp the fullness of the awareness of such a transformation,
our desire nurtures our reflection and engagement. As the
author and spiritual director Bruno Barnhart imagines,

Theology comes to life at its core with the simplicity, the immediacy, and the power that we have known in the New Testament. While we continue to develop our verbal interpretations, these continually dissolve and reconstitute in the simple central light of the mystery.[8]

The Complexities of Congregational Development

Given this desire for restoration, any sense of leadership within a spiritual community must anchor itself in this distinct unity, this *oneness* that is the mark of our true identity. All else in ministry and leadership—whether it be budgets, program development, or staff management—is derivative of and relative to our great concern for this oneness. As the theologian Martin Laird reminds us, when we discover and orient ourselves around the *unum necessarium*, the "one thing necessary" we encounter in Luke 10:42, we recognize again that "God is our homeland. And the homing instinct of the human being is homed on God."[9]

Yet so much in our practice of parish ministry draws our attention away from our primary focus on this oneness. While it is true that budgets must be crafted, staff must work together effectively, pastoral care must be given, and worship must be planned, we are called to ask ourselves how our particular awareness of ministry aligns with this primary concern for oneness. In this way, to return to where we began with the lunch conversation with my parish leader, a contemplative posture becomes a very aggressive matter when it questions the manner of approach within a community.

I think of church administration in particular. There can be a certain degree of autopilot when it comes to allocating the budget, planning the calendar, and responding to the concerns of the day. With the enormous amount of details that land on my desk—and on my parish administrator's desk—I am repeatedly convicted to ask myself, "How aware am I right now of how this particular detail connects to our primary concern for oneness?" It may sound trivial; I assure you it is not.

As the rector of a larger parish, I will be the first to say that we must have adequate administrative structures to ensure that we are effectively and faithfully organized as a community. Yet administration itself cannot be void of an attunement with the Spirit's living presence and guidance, of the deeper realization of our union with God and one another in Christ. Julia Gatta, my pastoral theology professor and doctoral thesis advisor at the School of Theology at the University of the South in Sewanee, Tennessee, often drew on the Methodist theologian Thomas Oden to make the point that within the very word *administration* one can find *ministry* hidden in plain sight. In Oden's words,

> Having borrowed heavily from programmatic management procedures while forgetting much of their traditional rootage, church administration has become an orphan discipline vaguely wondering about its true parentage.[10]

Such questions of administration, therefore, are deeply contemplative in nature, focusing as they do on our oneness in and with God in Christ. They are centered on both our deeper yearning for wholeness (the deep essence of salvation) and our propensity for egoic grasping that thwarts our desire. This contemplative posture of leadership calls us to turn our life away from an illusory self-preoccupation and toward the graceful embrace of the indwelling Spirit of God in Christ.

The Challenges of Pastoral Leadership

Within the heart of the busyness of community life, we can see how the vocation of leadership desperately needs the essential quality of contemplative silence. How else can we embark on such a trajectory toward this oneness that grounds our common mission? Again, Panikkar offers helpful and challenging words on this call to silence: "Often the immediate character of what is *urgent* distracts our attention from what is *important*."[11] For Panikkar, we lose sight of what is truly important, given the nature of our society and the anxieties we face. We are called to a practice of discernment in the midst of pressure, strain, and fixation that can only be facilitated by silence; yet silence, for Panikkar and the contemplative tradition, is not defined by the mere absence of noise but by a distinct posture of listening to the Spirit within life.

For some, the word *silence* can be a difficult word, with memories of trauma and being silenced. With this crucial pastoral dimension in mind, the Brown University professor and author Kevin Quashie invites us to explore the word *quiet* and its and meaning:

> Quiet is often used interchangeably with silence or stillness, but the notion of quiet [in the book] is neither motionless nor without sound. Quiet, instead, is a metaphor for the full range of one's inner life—one's desires, ambitions, hungers, vulnerabilities, fears.[12]

Panikkar speaks to this inner dimension as well: "The silence of life is that art of making silent the activities of life that are not life itself in order to reach the pure experience of life."[13] Both Panikkar's and Quashie's descriptions of the promise of a listening posture pertains directly to the dynamics of spiritual leadership: "Plunged into the activities of life, we lose the faculty of listening, and we alienate our-selves from our very source: Silence, God."[14]

This faculty of listening in and from silence is what con-nects us with our primary concern for the great oneness of our lives. It is silence that nurtures our common mission of restoration. This is why a contemplative practice is so essen-tial in leadership: it allows us to be aware of the myriad details of life without ever losing sight of the deeper nature of our existence in God. Given the details of parish leadership, I cannot imagine anything more aggressive than an intentional practice of holding silence—especially in a group of lawyers and financial experts!

Such a reflection on a contemplative posture that offers an alternative matrix in which a community can nurture its shared ministry is well and good on its own merits. How-ever, one may wonder how such a posture can be embodied. When we gathered for the New Contemplative Exchange at St. Benedict's Monastery, some of my colleagues wondered if such a reorientation was even possible within the institu-tional church. Has the traditional church community become so overly focused on programs that there is no room for such contemplative practice? Given what we have described in terms of the key elements of silence, listening, awareness, and transformation, what are the qualities within a community yearning for such a contemplative leadership?

In my experience, the embodiment of a contemplative pos-ture that seeks a more intentional grounding is marked by a vital understanding of *pressure* and *authority*. Every denomina-tional structure is different regarding how authority is shared between clergy and laity—especially regarding the relation-ship between the senior pastor and the fiduciary or governing board. Over time, every denomination developed out of certain historical contexts grounded in particular questions and tensions. In terms of administration, some denominations invest a great deal of authority in their senior clergy person while others invest more decision-making authority in an elected board. Tensions in leadership are experienced differently in each structure, and collaboration takes on different forms.

Despite the denominational differences, there is at least one common quality or dynamic when it comes to leadership—a dynamic that can easily be taken for granted: the clergy can always take a risk and charge committees and the community as a whole to focus their attention on a posture of prayer, listening, and dialogue that appreciates the vital role of silence. No matter the particular configuration of the decision-making system, a pastor who nurtures his or her own practice of prayer can always take a risk to call the entire community to prayer. The pastor can challenge and empower the community and exert a particular pressure that invites the community into a stance more receptive of the Spirit's guidance. The clergy can challenge the community to listen to one another and collaborate in a spirit of prayer.

To be sure, there will be resistance with this shift in posture. On one level, there may be the immediate ego-rooted tension around how to share in a collaboration that resists grasping and control within ministries. In addition, individual members of the parish may not feel they are spiritually adept or theologically articulate enough to face head-on a robust discussion of such a contemplative ethos that nurtures an awareness of our essential oneness. Members of the community may doubt their theological abilities, and, out of such anxiety, they may anxiously claim that such spiritual work and prayer is the responsibility of the clergy. However, my experience has shown that there is at least a seed of willingness to listen and work together within the community to share in faithful ministry. As John Main eloquently reminds us,

> Experiencing and verifying these truths [of the Christian faith] is not just the work of specialists in prayer. St. Paul's inspiring and exultant letters were not written to members of an enclosed religious Order, but to the ordinary butchers and bakers of Rome, Ephesus, and Corinth.[15]

I am not naïve about the propensity for egoic tendencies; rather, I am appreciative of a core willingness I have experienced in many people from diverse backgrounds to pause, listen, and trust.

With such a contemplative posture, the clergy can exert a particular and vital pressure that sets a tone for the entire community. Such a tone comes from a hermeneutic of appreciation and an anticipation that the Spirit is indeed at work in both the individual lives and the common life of the community. An ethos of silence and contemplative prayer nurtures a belief that God's yearning for our restoration is the reality that, indeed, fuels our own yearning for wholeness. As Tilden Edwards has often reminded me, it is no small thing to have a radical trust in the movement and power of the Holy Spirit. It is quite far-reaching to yield to the presence of the Spirit in our lives, to rest in an openness that anticipates God's presence. In his words,

> Within us there is a capacity for touching reality more directly than the thinking mind. It is activated when we're willing to let go of the thoughts that come through our mind and to sit in the spacious openness that appears between and behind them.[16]

Conclusion: A Brief Word on Desire

Perhaps we can begin to see the dynamics of spiritual leadership grounded in a contemplative awareness that holds as its primary focus the restoration of ourselves and the community to one another and to God. This is a leadership that remains focused on the essential oneness, keeping the myriad responsibilities of ministry in their relative and derivative positions. Such a pressure regarding leadership throughout the community must be anchored in a practice of prayer. The particular pressure clergy can exert is, in fact, an invitation for a community to share and live from its deepest desire. In terms of this desire, the monk and author Sebastian Moore offers a beautiful image:

> The key to Calvary is buried deep inside you, inside me: it is the same key that unlocks prayer, for it is desire. It is in some moment when you knew that nothing would ever satisfy you, and knew, at the same time, "This cannot be all there is!" Indeed we are far short of the desire that "for the sake of joy which lay ahead of him, endured the cross, disregarding the shame of it." But that is not the point. In fact the point is that we must be short of this. For this is desire, coming from a self that we hardly know as ours. It is seated in what mystics call *la pointe vierge*, the core of our being, when alone we may restore that image, blackened by the candle smoke of centuries.[17]

Thus it is not a pressure rooted in our own ego; rather, it is a pressure that is an echo of the Spirit's yearning for our wholeness and restoration. As the theologian Sarah Coakley describes, in such a contemplative posture

what is blanked out in the regular, patient attempt
to God in prayer is *any* sense of human grasp; and
what comes to replace such an ambition, over time, is
the elusive, but nonetheless ineluctable, sense of *being
grasped.*[18]

In this risky space of leadership, perhaps we can catch a
glimpse of what is possible in that reality of ultimate restoration: the kingdom of heaven so often envisioned by the
Gospel writers. The risk of failure is always present, no matter how one approaches the opportunities and demands of
leadership. Such a risk of failure is a mark of our contingent
humanity and our tendency toward ego and grasping. Yet
what would it be like to imagine a space of silence and contemplative prayer that resists the urge to maintain the status
quo, that presses against our temptation to control and grasp,
and that yields in trust to the Spirit of Christ who is always
within us? What if such a space of grace were possible—flaws
and all—here and now? Do we dare explore it?

Notes

1. As quoted in John Main, *Essential Writings* (Maryknoll, NY: Orbis
   Books, 2002), 63.
2. Richard J. Foster, *Celebration of Discipline: The Path to Spiritual Growth*
   (San Francisco: HarperSanFrancisco: 1978), 1.
3. *The Book of Common Prayer* (New York: Church Publishing, 1986),
   855.
4. There are myriad witnesses to our foundational oneness in God
   throughout the history of the Christian contemplative tradition. In
   particular, I have found Raimon Panikkar's insights important. See *The
   Experience of God: Icons of the Mystery* (Minneapolis: Fortress Press,
   2006). As well, Tilden Edwards speaks to the experience of union

within the community: "We share an inclusive sense of community with what is, because we find everyone and everything present and interrelated." *Embracing the Call to Spiritual Depth: Gifts for Contemplative Living* (Mahwah, NJ: Paulist Press, 2010), 7. See also John Main, *Essential Writings* (Maryknoll, NY: Orbis Books, 2002). Rowan Williams, as well, describes the experience of union within the Christian community, paying particular attention to the understanding of salvation by nurturing "the recognition that I do not go to heaven except in relation to those I serve and am served by in the Body of Christ, that what is given to me or to us is given for the whole." *On Christian Theology* (Malden, MA: Blackwell, 2000). This understanding of oneness, furthermore, finds its roots in the Patristic tradition. In particular, Pseudo-Dionysius speaks to this when he states, "Nothing in the world lacks its share in the One. Just as every number participates in unity—for we refer to one couple, one dozen, one-half, one-third, one-tenth—so everything, and every part of everything, participates in the One. By being the One, it is all things." *Pseudo-Dionysius: The Complete Works*, trans. Colm Luibheid, The Classics of Western Spirituality (Mahwah, NJ: Paulist Press, 1987), 128.

5. Eknath Easwaran, *Original Goodness* (Tomales, CA: Nilgiri Press, 1989), 17.

6. A. M. Allchin, *Participation in God: A Forgotten Strand in Anglican Tradition* (London: Darton, Longman, and Todd, 1988), 63.

7. Raimon Panikkar, *Christophany: The Fullness of Man* (Maryknoll, NY: Orbis Books, 2010), 21.

8. Bruno Barnhart, *The Future of Wisdom: Toward a Rebirth of Sapiential Christianity* (Rhinebeck, NY: Monkfish, 2018), 82.

9. Martin Laird, *Into the Silent Land: A Guide to the Christian Practice of Contemplation* (New York: Oxford University Press, 2006), 1–2.

10. Thomas Oden, *Pastoral Theology: Essentials of Ministry* (San Francisco: HarperCollins, 1983), 4. The particular reference for administration and ministry can be found on page 153.

11. Panikkar, *Experience of God*, 23.

12. Kevin Quashie, *The Sovereignty of Quiet: Beyond Resistance in Black Culture* (New Brunswick, NY: Rutgers University Press, 2012), 6.

13. Panikkar, *Experience of God*, 24.

14. Panikkar, 24.

15. John Main, *Word Into Silence: A Manual for Christian Meditation* (Norwich, UK: Canterbury Press, 2006), 6.

16. Edwards, *Embracing the Call to Spiritual Depth*, 9.

17. Sebastian Moore, *The Contagion of Jesus: Doing Theology as If It Mattered* (Maryknoll, NY: Orbis Books, 2007), 125.

18. Sarah Coakley, *God, Sexuality, and the Self: An Essay "On the Trinity"* (Cambridge, UK: Cambridge University Press, 2013), 23.

Creating Strategy with a Contemplative Ethos

KIRSTEN OATES

I was invited to attend the Snowmass gathering at St. Benedict's Monastery by Fr. Richard Rohr. The gathering was a catalysis for me to reflect on my own experiences of integrating a contemplative way of being into my daily life and work. I continue to develop these concepts in my role overseeing program design with the Center for Action and Contemplation (CAC) in Albuquerque, New Mexico.

Fr. Rohr founded the CAC in 1987, and has said many times that the most important word in the name of the organization is the word *and*:

> People have liked and affirmed our name from the very beginning. . . . We hoped it would keep us honest and force us toward balance and ongoing integration. Action as we are using the word does not mean activism, busyness, or "do-goodism." Action does mean a decisive commitment toward involvement and engagement in social order. Issues will not be resolved by mere reflection, discussion, or even prayer. God "works together with" all those who love (Rom 8:28). By contemplation we mean the deliberate seeking of God through a willingness to detach from

the passing self, the tyranny of emotions, the addiction to self-image and the false promises of the world. Contemplation is the "divine therapy" and the perennial clearinghouse. It is important that we continue to clarify and hold to these two pivots of our lives. Rightly sought, action and contemplation will always regulate, balance, and convert one another. Separately, they are dead-ended and trapped in personality. The clear goal of the Center is to meet people "where they are" and help them trust "where they are not." For all of us it is an endless rhythmic dance. The step changes now and then, but Someone Else always leads.[1]

Background

In 2015, I was employed by the CAC to support the executive director, Michael Poffenberger, in developing a strategy for the future of the organization. This piece of work coincided with my own personal desire to work with organizations where I could be more of a whole human being rather than a mere professional skill set. Fr. Richard teaches about the possibility of a contemplative way of being, seeing, and acting, and this particular chapter will reflect on the possibility of creating strategy grounded in a contemplative ethos. I will do this by drawing from my own experiences of being a strategic consultant to for-profit, nonprofit, and faith-based organizations, as well as reflecting on the strategic ethos that existed in those engagements. These prior contexts will then be contrasted with my experience of developing strategy with the CAC. I will end the chapter by offering some of the insights of the CAC strategic work and its implications for the organization going forward.

Strategy in the For-Profit Arena

My journey of working in the arena of strategy began with the opportunity to work as a consultant for a global firm serving for-profit organizations. *For-profit* means the primary goal of the business or organization is to make money (a profit). Back then, I was not following any kind of spiritual path. My desire was to develop a successful and rewarding career, and I seemed to be in a good position to achieve my dream. As a strategic consultant I worked on teams that supported large corporations by delivering successful strategies based in research, analysis, experience, and clear logic. The relationship between the consulting firm and the corporation would last anywhere from six months to many years of dedicated work. Consultants are asked to use all of their skills, attention, and effort to produce high-quality and effective results for whatever organization they are working with. It is a high-pressure environment, requiring long hours of work and, as I was told in orientation, "zero defects," even when there has been little time for sleep. I had the opportunity to work across a variety of industries, including banking, insurance, private equity, food and grocery, consumer goods, and airlines.

What I enjoyed most about the work was the team-oriented structure and creative collaboration with colleagues in solving challenging problems together. I also enjoyed going on-site with the corporations we were supporting to form relationships with the employees. Each of the organizations we worked with had their own value proposition and way of differentiating themselves in the market, but I experienced a common worldview that was at the heart of all the strategic work I did. That common thread was each organization's need to maximize shareholder value or profits. And while

I had no reason to question that worldview at the time, I started to feel what I believe are some of the symptoms of it. I was burning out, feeling drained and insecure, and I sensed a desire for something more "whole" for my life.

As I look back, it is clear to me how this underlying worldview impacts the way strategy is approached, created, and implemented. A corporation's executive director and board will be measured by the performance of the company's share price and the trajectory of its profits. Accountability lies solely with shareholders, and the determinate of success or failure is the value of a share. Therefore, pursuing gains in shareholder value is the most important function of the organization. This narrow frame impacts every aspect of the business. Strategy is created to maximize shareholder value, which leads to the allocation of resources and the creation of systems and roles to implement the strategy. The organization's accountability for its impact on customers, employees, the environment, and even the market it is cocreating is tethered to the more foundational accountability for share price. Put another way, the customer is valued based on the way they impact shareholder value; the employee is treated in ways that relate their value to their impact on shareholder value; and the corporation's impact on the environment is considered based on the way it impacts shareholder value. Corporations are enslaved to the financial markets that do not place a value on our underlying sacred wholeness and oneness with the world and all beings. When I discussed this with the author and retreat leader James Finley, he reflected that "the free markets are not free because shareholder value is not shared in a way that recognizes who we really are."[2] The free markets are not congruent with our God-given sense of freedom within the context of our connectedness.

Strategy in the Nonprofit Arena

Without the benefit of these kinds of insights at the time, I hoped a shift to the nonprofit world would solve my symptoms. Nonprofits organize and operate solely to fulfill a charitable mission and pay no income tax on the donations they receive or any money they earn through fundraising activities. After working for fifteen years in the for-profit sector, I began working with large nonprofit organizations with missions I could believe in. The major strategic questions were markedly different from the ones in the for-profit world, and I expanded my skills and tools as I worked with organizations doing heroic work in the community. However, I began to experience a lack of congruency between the externalized missional zeal and the internal reality of working for those organizations. Looking back, I believe that just like in the for-profit sector, there is an underlying worldview that leads to this kind of dysfunction.

When you are doing strategy for a nonprofit organization, you generally begin by identifying a particular need in the community they serve or could serve, as well as a desired outcome that stems from that need being met. The mission of the organization is directly tied to serving that particular need and contributing to that outcome. A well-known example of this is Boys and Girls Clubs of America, whose mission is "to enable all young people, especially those who need us most, to reach their full potential as productive, caring, responsible citizens."[3] Any strategy developed by consultants, the directors, and the board articulates how the organization will most effectively serve the need given accessible resources. It defines "who needs us most" and exactly how the organization will help them reach "full potential." The organization creates systems and roles to implement the strategy as well as ways to measure the results.

This is important work, but in my experience the world-view is too narrow. It is based on one particular need that certainly benefits from this type of attention, but that one need is not articulated in relation to the whole. I have worked with organizations where the executive director is passionately focused on serving the external community need while running riot over the very real needs of the organization's staff. The narrow need-based worldview is often permeated with a sense of scarcity as a result of the competitive and difficult nature of fundraising. This sense of scarcity creates further stress within nonprofit organizations that aim to address massive community problems. In the end, working in the nonprofit sector was evoking the same draining sensations I felt working for organizations in the for-profit world, and I was disheartened.

Strategy in the Mainline Church

At this point in my career, my desire for a more "whole" life led me on a spiritual path to Christianity. My particular practice began in the Anglican Church, where I experienced an initial conversion. Not too long after, I took a different trajectory in my career and began consulting with faith-based organizations. This was initially a valuable pairing because it is rare that churches take time to think strategically about how to best implement their vision and use their resources most effectively. Pastors tend to be passionate about pastoring or teaching and not so passionate about managing their staff and organization. However, the deeper I stepped into the mainline church's worldview, the more I recognized it was also fragmented. Fr. Richard talks about the church tending to reinforce our "illusion of separateness and finiteness, which in turn causes us to split: shadow self from idealized self, mind from body and soul, life from death, ourselves from other selves and the natural world."[4] In theological terms, the majority of the mainline church's worldview is grounded in original sin rather than original blessing, and such an orientation holds us in a transactional state of judgment and separateness from God instead of participating in the flow of God's love. This overarching frame creates a need for us to reject who we are, making it impossible to create programs that are built on the sacredness of all life, that allow people to be vulnerable and free to participate with wholeness in the world.

Strategy with a Contemplative Organization

Finally, my searching for wholeness led me to the work of Fr. Richard, and I started to feel as if what I longed for was possible. I dove deep into his teaching and eventually became a student of the CAC's Living School for Action and Contemplation.[5] The school is based on a heritage of faith from what we at the CAC call the "Christian contemplative living lineage," also known as the "Christian mystical tradition," which operates in respect of all other wisdom traditions. The core faculty is Richard Rohr, Cynthia Bourgeault, and James Finley.

The Christian contemplative or mystical lineage is a historical stream of Christianity within the overarching Christian tradition. Fr. Richard has called it the lineage of spiritual wisdom, and it has been carried forward through the lives and teachings of Christian mystics and theologians. Fr. Richard states, "This tradition is the much older and more solid tradition, and from it we can again be taught."[6] In terms of this mystical element within the broader Christian tradition, Fr. Richard has defined a mystic as "one who has moved from mere belief systems or belonging systems to actual inner experience. All traditions agree that such a movement is possible, desirable, and available to everyone. In fact, Jesus seems to say that this is the whole point! (Jn 10:19–38)."[7]

This lineage offers a description of the life force of all creation as God or Love as well as a path for experiencing (in an embodied way) union with this Love and with all of reality. The thirteenth-century theologian and mystic Meister Eckhart put it this way in one of his sermons: "The eye through which I see God is the same eye through which God sees me; my eye and God's eye are one eye, one seeing, one knowing, one love."[8]

The path to this kind of embodied union is shown to us in the universal pattern that is captured in the biblical narrative of Jesus's life, death, and resurrection. The journey is not linear but cyclical, and it encourages practices or experiences of knowing as well as not-knowing in an ever-deepening surrender (or death) of our ego-based habits and needs to Love or God. This journey is nurtured by a daily practice that invites grace to awaken us to an ever-deepening experience of the living presence of God in us and in the world, one with all of our limits and pains. Growing in our ability to surrender our ego and our will to God's love leads to "a decisive commitment toward involvement and engagement in social order. God 'works together with' all those who love (Rom 8:28)."[9]

Being educated about this ancient worldview enabled me to see why, to date, I was unable to find a way to wholeness in my career. It became clear that organizations that are not grounded in a worldview of oneness and wholeness not necessarily limited to a religion—detract from our innate desire to live in congruency to this wholeness that underlies our reality.

The for-profit world focuses on *getting* rather than *being*. The nonprofit world tries to address the ways the world both lacks equality and creates suffering by serving unserved needs. While such work can be a positive contribution, it is often done based on a sense of scarcity and separateness, and it can lead to burn out and competition instead of collaboration. Many churches, as well, contribute to a belief system that ignores wholeness and oneness, and staff can become cynical and hardened to their innate desire for bringing their whole selves into connection with God. Change will not come about easily to any of these sectors because this is not just a matter of doing things differently. The transformative shift we are speaking of requires seeing reality differently from a different consciousness.

> What is it that keeps us humans from reading reality truthfully, humbly, and helpfully? Why do we—including people at the highest levels of church, education, and state—appear to be so imprisoned in ourselves? In effect, why have the world religions stopped doing their job of spiritually transforming people and cultures? Why have we told people they must "believe" God in order to experience God, when God is clearly at work in ways that many "eyes have not seen, nor ears have heard, nor has entered into our minds" (1 Cor 2:9)? . . . Wisdom is precisely the freedom to be present.[10]

Cynthia Bourgeault says that Jesus came to help people awaken, "but awakening is not that easy, and as a *moshel meshalim* [master of wisdom], Jesus had mixed success. As the four Gospels all record, some people glimpsed what he was saying while others missed it altogether. Some people got it part of the time and missed it the rest. Some people woke up and others remained asleep."[11]

Given this particular trajectory in my own life and practice, I got my chance to try to do things differently when I began my work of developing a strategic plan for the CAC. The goal of the strategic plan was to answer this question: Is there life for the CAC beyond the life of its founder, Fr. Richard? Should the organization try to carry something forward beyond Fr. Richard's life, or should it simply become a static place where his legacy is held? Given Fr. Richard's age, the answer would set the trajectory for the organization over the coming years. The starting point was to note that although the CAC had done a number of things over its thirty-year history, it was primarily known and supported as a vehicle for dispersing Fr. Richard's work in the world.

For me, working with the CAC was an opportunity to create strategy grounded in a sense of wholeness because this contemplative tradition describes God and our ultimate reality as whole. I had longed for such a coherence between strategy and reality throughout my entire career. My approach was to try to hold two concurrent practices. First, I would use my efforts, skills, and experience to define, analyze, and answer the strategic questions at hand. Second, I would personally be embodied in a sense of "not knowing" and vulnerable surrender to the presence of God participating in all reality, always generous, loving, and whole.

A Personal and Professional Turning Point

This was new territory for me, and I wasn't quite sure how to approach it, but my personal life offered an experience that I would draw on during those first conversations and into the work. About six months prior to starting this work, my sister-in-law, Meg, went into the hospital for what was supposed to be a fairly minor heart surgery. However, once the doctors began the operation, they discovered too late that her heart was in much worse shape than they had realized. As a result, she almost died during the operation, and she came out of the surgery into intensive care on a ventilator and with a difficult path ahead.

Meg had one son, William, who was twenty-one at the time and had just graduated from college. Meg and Will had been a family of two since Will was very young, and he was there in the hospital to support his mom each day. Meg had a strong desire to live, and she kept asking the doctors to give her a plan, to save her life. It was unfathomable to all of us that they might not be able to help her, but after four months in intensive care, Meg's heart muscles were still not functioning properly and as a result her organs began to fail.

Two days after Christmas 2014, we knew Meg was close to death, and Will and her family were by her side all day. Late that evening, after everyone else had left, Will, committed to staying with his mom, set himself up on the couch in her room with a blanket and a pillow. I also felt drawn to stay, and I made myself a makeshift bed between two office chairs next to Will. The three of us lay together in the dark. Will and I talked about his mom and his dad, and then he shared that his greatest fear in life had always been the fear of losing his mom. He didn't know what he was going to do. In that moment I told him that, although I didn't know what he was going to do either, I knew he would not be alone. Late into the night, Will fell asleep, and I lay there in the dark with the sounds of the hospital machines echoing around me. My heart began to ache like it was too big for my chest and the pain kept getting worse. I thought I might be having a heart attack, but then I had a vision of Meg emptying all of the love she held in her heart for her son into my heart. At one point my heart was in so much pain I internally shouted out to Meg, "I don't think I can take any more, but I promise you I've got him." With tears in my eyes I bowed my ego to something that seemed illogical and unbelievable but at the same time completely present, loving, and trustworthy. I surrendered my heart to this love and my heart was transformed, along with my entire being, to feel the joy and pain of a mother's love and be responsive to love's demands.

Meg died the next morning, but her mother's love filled my heart and still does to this day. As sweet and transformative as that has been for me, I hold it in humble regard for the tragic loss of a mother, sister, and daughter who longed to stay with us. I live in a daily commitment to continue to surrender to the love that animated Meg's heart and now animates mine, so I can be there for Will like a mother, come what may.

Not long after Meg died, I started working on the CAC strategy. Each day I tried to bring all of my skill and expertise to bear while holding myself in a state of openhearted vulnerability similar to what I had experienced in the hospital. With the support of the executive director and board chair, I attempted to build processes and ways of working together that were more aligned to the contemplative way. How we did everything mattered just as much as what we produced. Our shared decision-making process began with a commitment to a daily practice of contemplative meditation. It included practices such as passionately arguing for insights while letting go of any attachment to them as either right, necessary, or proving our worth. We spent time with wisdom elders in the field of spirituality listening deeply to what was arising in them as they sat with our questions. We asked constituents to reflect back to us how we are experienced in our engagements with them. We shared in each other's lives so that our work didn't feel separate from our ability to be a whole human being committed to a contemplative path. Fr. Richard's deep knowledge and experience, as well as his contemplative presence, were grounding forces for this work.

Insights from CAC's Strategy

From this space of contemplative grounding, we faced the painful and anxious reality of the broader institution of the Christian church. Research and interviews pointed to the church and seminary being in a period of decline. These institutions are, for the most part, unable to support deeper levels of spiritual formation and are not remaining relevant to the needs of the community. Many people leaving the church (or not entering it) remain drawn to a spiritual life and want substance, discipline, and community based in a tradition, but have few outlets for finding it outside the institutional church. For millennials, the search for new forms of spirituality, community, and a sense of meaning is particularly pronounced. They are skeptical of institutions and tend to be nonhierarchical in how they network and organize themselves. Alongside this decline in the traditional church, technology is giving people unprecedented access to wisdom teachers across traditions. While many are using this capacity to find teaching and develop a spiritual path for themselves, they often long for a sense of belonging to community and recognize the limits of going it alone. In the workplace, some organizations are offering mindfulness training and meditation, and while this might lead to lower stress and greater productivity, it is not necessarily leading to a more compassionate, loving world.[12]

While it appears that there is no clear or consistent path forward for how traditional spiritual communities will change or develop in the future, the CAC believes "there is increasing recognition that the nondual, contemplative, mystical is the only way out for Christianity."[13] Through surveys and focus groups, CAC constituents described the impact of Fr. Richard and the contemplative lineage on which the CAC grounds its continued opportunities. The core elements shared by these focus groups include being able to commit to a Christian path and grow in their faith; committing to contemplative practices that positively affect their lives; experiencing positive changes in relationships, behaviors, and beliefs; and finding the ability to navigate the circumstances of their lives.

One of Fr. Richard's responses to the current challenging landscape was to create the Living School for Action and Contemplation. Fr. Richard initially talked about the school as a kind of underground contemplative seminary in response to the fact that

> as of now, not a single denominational seminary has been able to [incorporate contemplation into their curriculum]. . . . Contemplative epistemology and theology are seen as superficial add-ons rather than the core of the matter. Which might help to explain, at least in part, why so many churches are losing members so rapidly![14]

Experts in our field recognized the value of this initiative and its potential to influence the landscape in positive ways longer term. The Living School is a collaborative model, bringing together three exemplary teachers who have been recognized in their own right as embodying wisdom. It uses technology but also recognizes the importance of in-person transmission.

We asked experts and constituents the original question of whether the CAC should continue beyond the life of its founder, and we heard a resounding yes! In a recent conversation, James Finley put it this way: "Although the CAC at one level is about Richard, Richard isn't about Richard, so the CAC needs to carry forward what Richard is about: the Christian contemplative lineage with respect for all other wisdom lineages."[15] With all of our findings in mind, we are moving forward with the desire to continue the work of the CAC, and we have established a set of strategic goals that are grounded in a contemplative ethos. We hope to articulate the Christian contemplative lineage more systematically; strengthen the school; expand our programs, teachers, and forms of engagement; create more intentional pathways for people who desire to go deeper; and develop ways of supporting the broader community of people and organizations grounded in the contemplative tradition who are committed to contemplative engagement and awakening in the world.

Within our ongoing strategic development, we also recognize that one of the current shadows of this broader contemplative tradition is the lack of diverse voices being represented and supported. As a majority white organization, we feel an urgent need to address the ways we might be perpetuating white domination paradigms. For us, unearthing our shadow isn't about political correctness; rather, it speaks to the ways we are hindered from the reality of our oneness within God, the grounding dynamic of our lives. Fr. Richard notes that

> White privilege is largely hidden from our eyes if we
> are white. Why? Because it is structural instead of

psychological, and we tend to interpret most things
in personal, individual, and psychological ways. . . .
Because we have never been on the other side, we
largely do not recognize the structural access, the trust
we think we deserve, the assumption that we always
belong and do not have to earn our belonging, the
"we set the tone" mood that we white folks live inside
of—and take totally for granted and even naturally
deserved. Only the outsider can spot all these attitudes
in us. . . . In my opinion, "whiteness" loves order
above all else (not love), and has used the scriptures
to enforce its version of order: Christendom itself, the
Crusades, the Inquisition, the genocide of the Ameri-
cas, slavery, apartheid, unjust voting rights and voting privileges, the noneducation of women and blacks
were all justified by the Bible, and most especially by
Bible thumpers![16]

Our Worldview Sets Our Path

We have experienced that there is a possibility of creating
strategy grounded in a contemplative ethos. However, that
possibility is much more like the nature of the contemplative
path, which includes both effort and surrender. The contemplative path is not stipulated. Instead, it comes as our life,
and the way we become contemplative is in a humility of
surrender of anything and everything that gets in the way of
God's ever-present love. The contemplative path is grounded
in a worldview of oneness so that a connection to God's ever-
present love is experienced as a deep connection and love for
the sacredness of the whole, everything in existence. While

individuals may be pursuing this path, organizations are caught in worldviews and structures that lead to strategies and cultures focused on separateness, greed, and exclusion. The CAC's strategic process had the benefit of Fr. Richard's years of commitment to this path, as well as a desire for the strategy to be based in his contemplative worldview. This rootedness and yearning was combined with the strategic tools and experience of the executive director and me and our own humility to know that we don't know as we keep surrendering to the way Love emerges.

Notes

1. Richard Rohr, "Not the Center for Activism & Introspection," *Radical Grace* 4, no. 6 (December 1991–January 1992).

2. Dr. James Finely, personal communication, April 22, 2018.

3. "Our Mission and Story," Boys and Girls Clubs of America, accessed May 15, 2018, https://www.bgca.org/about-us/our-mission-story.

4. From the CAC's Future State Vision, approved by the CAC board in July 2016.

5. A description of the school can be found at "Living School," Center for Action and Contemplation, accessed May 25, 2018, https://cac.org/living-school/living-school-welcome.

6. Richard Rohr, *The Naked Now: Learning to See as the Mystics See* (New York: Crossroad, 2009), 33.

7. Rohr, *Naked Now*, 30.

8. Meister Eckhart, *Qui Audit Me,* sermon on Sirach 24:30. See *The Complete Mystical Works of Meister Eckhart*, trans. and ed. Maurice O'C. Walshe (New York: Crossroad, 2009), 298.

9. Richard Rohr, "Not the Center for Activism & Introspection," *Radical Grace* 4, no. 6, (December 1991–January 1992).

10. Rohr, *Naked Now*, 10–11.

11. Cynthia Bourgeault, *The Wisdom Way of Knowing: Reclaiming an Ancient Tradition to Awaken the Heart* (San Francisco: John Wiley, 2003), 5.

12. Ute Kreplin, Miguel Farias, and Inti A. Brazil, "The Limited Prosocial Effects of Meditation: A Systematic Review and Meta-Analysis," *Scientific Reports* 8, no. 1 (February 2018): doi:10.1038/s41598-018-20299-z.

13. Richard Rohr, From the CAC's Future State Vision, approved by the CAC board in July 2016.

14. Richard Rohr, *Essential Teachings on Love* (New York: Orbis Books, 2018).

15. Dr. James Finely, personal communication, September 20, 2015.

16. Romal J. Tune, "Richard Rohr on White Privilege," Sojourners, January 19, 2016, https://sojo.net/articles/richard-rohr-white-privilege.

Imaginative Contemplation and the Gift of Compassion

BO KAREN LEE

My first experience of Buddhist meditation occurred at an American Academy of Religion conference, during a session of the Contemplative Studies Group,[1] where a Buddhist scholar guided about sixty of us through a "compassion meditation."[2] The presenter invited us to select a compassion figure from our lives and to sit with this person—or even a pet animal, if a person could not be found—in our mind's eye. Determined to honor the practice and not slide into Christian prayer, I chose my mother, who throughout my life had been the source of the deepest unconditional love I had received from any human being. Waves of compassion washed over me, and my soul expanded with her love. And then, unwelcomed and uninvited, Christ came rushing into my imagination, because I had experienced in him a compassion and love that infinitely outweighed the greatest love my mother could give me. Embarrassed at first by his appearance, I could no longer hide that Christ was to me a fountain of compassion and kindness, so I chose to stop suppressing this wellspring of love in my life.[3]

This tender "intrusion" from Christ resonates, I believe, with C. S. Lewis's experience penning *The Chronicles of Narnia*, a classic series of children's novels. He explains that he

111

had originally envisioned the story without a trace of Aslan, the noble lion who in his completed series serves as the main hero and redemption figure. But in one moment, as Lewis put it, "suddenly, Aslan came bounding into it" and changed everything.[4] And so too Christ came bounding into my imagination with surprising immediacy and gentle compassion during the American Academy of Religion meeting, and in my life he has changed everything.

Compassion and the Academy

Mary Rose O'Reilley notes in her book *The Peaceable Classroom* that one question kept returning to her as a young teacher: "Is it possible to teach English so that people stop killing each other?"[5] A related question drives my pedagogical explorations: Is it possible to teach [whatever subject we teach] so that we engender more compassion in the world? And while I have cherished learning from my Buddhist colleagues, might the Christian tradition also have rich resources to offer toward greater healing for both professors and students?

One form of Christian prayer that has surprised me in the classroom is that which employs Ignatian imagination, or "Gospel contemplation," a way of prayer based on the life and writings of St. Ignatius of Loyola (1491–1556), founder of the Jesuit Order. There is resonance between this form of prayer and the meditation through which my Buddhist colleague led us; and while the external structure of prayer is similar (e.g., focus on a compassion figure in your mind's eye, and let their compassion reach you), the content of the meditation between the two traditions varies widely. In many of the conversations among our colleagues in the Contemplative Studies Group, as well as the Association for the Contemplative Mind in Higher Education, insights from Eastern traditions were presented, with little representation from the Christian contemplative tradition. But if one of our shared purposes is to bring more compassion into the world, I would like to explore how Christian meditation can be a source of encounter with a loving God who births more compassion into the hearts of Christ's followers.[6] Unfortunately, this kind of compassion is not always evident in the academy, even among (or sometimes especially among) Christian theologians. In this essay, I invite you to meander with me through several more experiences that shifted my understanding of compassion and its place in the academy; I ask your patience (this kind of genre is new to me as a writer)—you will eventually understand my intention and what I am trying to bring into my classroom and potentially into yours.

As a scholar, I have wrestled with the pressing task of bringing compassion explicitly into my academic discourse— and also with stewarding our shared academic work to increase compassion in the world. Compassion here can be understood as "loving concern for another," or more literally, "co-suffering" ("to suffer with").[7] And compassion is an especially important trait for students in my context—that is, seminarians (future ministers)—to cultivate. While teaching at Loyola College, I rejoiced to learn that the virtue of intellectual charity was championed among my colleagues, faithful to the Jesuit tradition—that it was possible (and recommended!) to be kind and gracious in listening to another's arguments, whether or not I agreed with them. In the larger academy, however, compassion and academic rigor often seemed at odds with each other. The more pointed a scholarly discussion was, the more coldly analytic it tended to be. And a desire to win the argument can outweigh the shared purpose of coming to a deeper understanding of the subject matter together. When our academic work is meant, ultimately, to serve the larger good—even to bring a measure of healing to the world—this disconnect becomes rather disorienting.

One profound enactment of this dissonance occurred at another American Academy of Religion conference: scholars rushed off to hear a big-name ethicist wax eloquent on the importance of social justice issues in our day. As we raced to this meeting, I noticed that the majority of us walked right past several homeless people we encountered on the street, treating them as barriers to our agenda rather than precious (fellow) members of the human race. The parable of the good Samaritan came immediately to mind. When did I become a self-righteous religious leader (theologian)? And when (and how) did our academic pontifications stop serving our human community? As the character Ivan confesses to his younger brother Alyosha in Fyodor Dostoyevsky's *The Brothers Karamazov*, "I love humanity" (as a matter of theory and moral principle). But when the neighbor shows up with that "stupid, smelly face," all love is gone.[8] We theologians seem often to have more of Ivan than the kindly Samaritan within us.

Pathways to Compassion

Academia, of course, is not utterly devoid of compassion; it can be a source of compassion as well. What, then, might this look like in the classroom or in scholarly discussions, when one's neighbor is a student or a colleague? Another experience I had (again, alongside Buddhist colleagues) revealed a potential way forward. During a conference on "Moral Injury and Collective Healing,"[9] I was struck by the depth of compassion present among both the leaders and participants of the workshop, a workshop that included its fair share of scholars from both Eastern and Western religious traditions. Scholars (including theologians and ethicists), teachers, physicians, chaplains (military, prison, etc.), counselors, meditation practitioners, and others in various care professions gathered to discuss pathways of healing for those suffering from various wounds of trauma and moral injury. Stirred by the presentations, I was compelled to explore sources and inspirations for this compassion, and so I had personal conversations with several of the workshop leaders in which we pondered streams of compassion in one another's lives. What makes a person loving and open toward others, and what helps them—what helps us—to truly care about the pain that others experience?[10]

I identified two sources of compassion through these conversations. One important source seemed to be the suffering one has endured in one's own life.[11] As Rabbi Joachim Prinz put it in 1963, expressing the solidarity of the Jewish people with the civil rights movement, "It is not merely sympathy and compassion for the Black people of America that motivates us, it is above all and beyond such sympathies and emotions a sense of complete identification and *solidarity born of our own painful historic experiences*."[12]

The theologian and civil rights leader Howard Thurman conveys a similar insight:

> *I share with you the agony of your grief,*
> *The anguish of your heart finds echo in my own.*
> I know I cannot enter all you feel
> Nor bear with you the burden of your pain;
> I can but offer what my love does give:

The strength of caring,
The warmth of one who seeks to understand
The silent storm-swept barrenness of so great a loss,
This I do in quiet ways,
That on your lonely path
You may not walk alone.[13]

One question that arises, then, is how one cultivates genuine concern for others when one has not experienced significant suffering in one's own life?

A second source of compassion that emerged was the depth of compassion that one has received in one's own life. If one has not experienced compassion from others, there is naturally less compassion to share. And here is where the gift of meditation lies. In personal meditation practices, one is opened up to experiencing the love of God, or compassion from other sources, which grows compassion and instincts for service in the practitioner.[14] Writing from within a Christian perspective, for example, the Catholic theologian Henri Nouwen has argued that solitude is the furnace of transformation within which compassion is birthed, because one meditates intentionally on God's love for self and for others. He also explains that without "solitude we remain victims of our society and continue to be entangled in the illusions of the false self," seeking applause and approval from fleeting, unreliable sources.[15] This search then implodes upon us. I have become increasingly convinced that it is nearly impossible to extend compassion to others when one has not first received it deeply from another source, namely, from "compassion figures" who fill our hearts with love, self-acceptance, courage, and kindness.

Returning to the first source of compassion above, how does one grow in compassion for others when their suffering eludes one's own experience? And can those who have led relatively sheltered, privileged lives, for example, enter with genuine solidarity into others' pain? Fr. Gregory Boyle, author of *Tattoos on the Heart*, gave an apt response to this very question during a recent lecture at Princeton University.[16] Turning in particular to the gift of Ignatian meditation, Fr. Boyle explained that if one can enter into fellowship with Christ, the supremely compassionate one who bore the sufferings of the world in his own body, then one can stand together with him in *his* solidarity with others.[17] In the words of Henri Nouwen,

> To pray for others means to make them part of ourselves. To pray for others means to allow their pains and sufferings, their anxieties and loneliness, their confusion and fears to resound in our innermost selves. To pray, therefore is to become those for whom we pray, to become the sick child, the fearful mother. . . .To pray is to enter into a deep inner solidarity with our fellow human beings so that in and through us they can be touched by the healing power of God's spirit. . . . When, as disciples of Christ, we are able to bear the burdens of our brothers and sister, to be marked with their wounds, and even be broken by their sins, our prayer becomes their prayer, our cry for mercy becomes their cry. In compassionate prayer, we bring before God those who suffer not merely "over there" . . . but here and now in our innermost selves.[18]

Whether through meditation and prayer or other avenues of spiritual practice, one is able to enter into fellowship with Christ's sufferings, and thereby with the world's suffering. If I "place myself with Christ," as Ignatius of Loyola put it, I place myself also with my neighbors' sorrows, as Christ, the man of sorrows, places himself in solidarity with them.[19] As the philosopher Nicholas Wolterstorff elaborates:

> For a long time, I knew that God is not the impassive, unresponsive, unchanging being portrayed by the classical theologians. I knew of the pathos of God. . . . But strangely, his suffering I never saw before. God is not only the God of the sufferers but *the God who suffers*. The pain and fallenness of humanity have entered into his heart. Through the prism of my tears, I have seen a suffering God. . . . Instead of explaining our suffering God shares it. But I never saw it. Though I confessed that the man of sorrows was God himself, I never saw the God of sorrows. . . . And great mystery: to redeem our brokenness and lovelessness, the God who suffers with us did not strike some mighty blow of power but sent his beloved son to suffer like us, through his suffering to redeem us from suffering and evil.[20]

This source of compassion has been overlooked in some contemplative circles, and this chapter focuses on retrieving Ignatian meditation as a significant resource for meditators, both inside and outside the classroom.[21] Not only does Ignatius teach contemplatives how to place themselves "with Christ" in solidarity with others, he also leads the pray-er into deeper experiences of Christ's compassion, both for the pray-er and for the ones for whom the pray-er prays. While many wisdom traditions teach compassion meditations, if Ignatian prayer is excluded from that wider array of meditation practices, a powerful source of compassion will be lost and our collective wisdom diminished. I seek in this essay to restore the distinctive contributions of the Ignatian tradition to the larger conversations within contemplative studies.

The Spiritual Exercises: *A Pathway to Deepening Compassion*

The genius of Ignatius of Loyola's *Spiritual Exercises* lies in the way it opens avenues for meditators to come face-to-face with the person of Jesus Christ and the depth of his compassion toward them and others.[22] I was first introduced to practices of Ignatian prayer when I taught at Loyola College (now University) in Maryland, and dove further into its riches when I started teaching Christian spirituality at Princeton Theological Seminary. My interest was especially piqued when a colleague of mine, who had been a Catholic priest for thirty years, made the startling comment that he had served his parish for all those years without once ever encountering Christ himself—until he prayed through the *Spiritual Exercises*. In fact, as Henri Nouwen admitted of himself in *The Return of the Prodigal Son*, many ministers and theologians, even while proclaiming the love of Christ to others, remain perpetual bystanders to that love—the unhappy plight of the firstborn son in the parable—rather than knowing themselves to be deeply beloved as the prodigal child.[23] Ignatius illumines one valuable pathway from bystander to beloved, bringing the pray-er into a more immediate experience of the compassionate Christ.

As a new teacher of spirituality at Princeton Seminary, I was surprised when, on a five-day class retreat at Bethany Spirituality Center, several of my students recounted experiences similar to my Catholic priest colleague. They had studied Gospel narratives and some could masterfully exegete the

Greek text. But few had deeply encountered the Christ whom they hoped to serve. Sister Stella Herrera, one of our retreat directors, facilitated group Ignatian spiritual reading in a way that I had myself never experienced, and my students too were in for a treat. Christ came face-to-face with this unsuspecting group of seminarians, and in witnessing their intimate encounters with Christ, I too experienced God's compassion anew.

Before turning to the internal dynamic of Ignatius of Loyola's prayer manual, *The Spiritual Exercises*—a manual primarily for spiritual directors seeking to aid others in their journey of prayer—I offer a brief word on his spiritual biography.[24] With a thirst for high adventure, Ignatius of Loyola pursued one thing: glory. A cannonball during a battle in Pamplona arrested his course. Mandatory convalescence brought this young knight face to face with nothing but spiritual books. Though Ignatius sought his beloved romance novels during his recovery, only two books were available to him: *The Life of Christ* and *The Lives of the Saints*. And so Ignatius encountered the figure of Jesus Christ, who captivated his imagination and reset his life—even as vanity had in the past moved him to reset his own leg (by asking surgeons to break and reset it, so that he would look good in his tights) when it had healed less than beautifully.

The resetting of Ignatius' life was equally drastic and at times painful. His new journey led him to a deep depression when he subjected himself to harsh practices. After a year of angst and suffering, he experienced sacred presence "in all things" at the bubbling brook in Manresa. Ignatius realized that God wanted his loving companionship not through practices of self-mortification alone, but through the beauty of children's laughter, women chatting over laundry, and the natural world. Ignatius discovered a new freedom and a "greater glory."[25]

Passion, though now of a different nature, continued to pulsate through Ignatius' spiritual pursuits. As the leader of a new movement (the Society of Jesus, or the Jesuits), he famously encouraged Francis Xavier to "set the world on fire." And a popular little Jesuit prayer book has the fitting title, "Hearts on Fire."[26] (One of my favorite stories of Ignatius' life comes from one of his fellow Jesuits, who "caught" him kneeling on the roof of the community house in which the early Jesuits lived. How strange it might have been for Ignatius' young comrade to find his leader secretly at prayer, with tears flowing down his cheeks, hands raised and eyes lifted toward the moonlit sky, apparently moved by nothing other than divine love.[27]

This devotion seems to be at the core of what makes Ignatius' prayer manual, *The Spiritual Exercises*, widely helpful to the Christian church, and even to the contemplative classroom.[28] The manner in which Ignatius translated his love of romance novels into his newly imaginative reading of *The Life of Christ*[29] (and later the Gospels) seems to find expression in these *Exercises,* bringing the pray-er right into the scene. Together with the first generation of disciples who encountered the risen Christ on the road to Emmaus, hearts often "burn within" through the gift of Ignatian prayer. And so students of Ignatius, even today, often find their eyes opening to the presence of Christ, previously hidden from their spiritual perception. They develop a personal relationship with Christ, by imagining themselves with Jesus in various parts of the Gospel. In this way, the Gospel is "lived" as much as "read."

The Spiritual Exercises is comprised of four movements (or "weeks"), each of which brings the retreatant into an

encounter with the compassionate Christ. In the first movement, the individual ponders the beauty of the created world,
alongside its brokenness, and reflects particularly on oneself
as profoundly beloved of God. One basks in the compassion
of Christ and learns to love oneself, extending that compassion to oneself even in the midst of life's severe woundings. In
the second movement, the pray-er meditates on the incarnation, life, and ministry of Christ, walking alongside him as he
brings healing and compassion to others. In the third movement, the retreatant accompanies Christ through his passion,
daring to stay with him in his suffering as he suffered alongside others. In the fourth and final movement, the retreatant
witnesses the resurrection and the power of the risen life.
Ignatius's distinctive way of prayer involves a vivid use of the
imagination, in which retreatants place themselves within the
Gospel narrative, almost as if part of a motion picture.[30]

Sister Stella did not lead us through the four-week journey of the *Spiritual Exercises*,[31] but we prayed through some
of the scriptures of the second movement (the life and ministry of Christ) using Ignatian imagination, or what followers of Ignatius call the method of "Gospel contemplation."[32]
Trained and steeped in Ignatian spirituality, Sister Stella led us
through the story of the hemorrhaging woman (Mk 5:21–34),
inviting us to make the scene contemporary to our context.
She also asked us to place ourselves in the scene. With which
character did we relate? Where were we, physically, in relation to the character of Jesus? What might Jesus have said
directly to us, to me, in this unfolding scene? With the motion
picture rolling forward, were we one of the disciples trying to
protect Jesus from being crushed by the crowd? (As one student added, "Was I merely there out of curiosity, thirsty for
novelty, or genuinely intrigued?") Were we one of the crowd,

pressing in, desperate for a loving glance or for healing? Or were we—was I, perhaps—the woman who suffered from twelve years of unceasing blood flow, who received the gift of telling Jesus her "whole story"?[33]

In small group discussion afterward, one student relayed her encounter with the story and her experience *within* the story. Identifying with the hemorrhaging woman, she explained that during the third reading of the narrative she experienced what she could only call "a surge of power" going through her physical frame; in that moment of the woman reaching out for the hem of Jesus' garment, the anxiety she had carried with her to the retreat lifted. Her countenance had indeed changed, as well as her focus: she now wanted to hear how her classmates were doing and to bear their burdens, no longer angling for comfort for herself. A few weeks later, she explained to me that she had been struggling with a physical ailment prior to the retreat and that since the retreat, doctors told her that her condition had reversed itself.[34] These kinds of stories are well above my paygrade as a teacher in theological education; but after hearing this one, I knew that I needed to pay attention to this form of Ignatian spiritual reading in my subsequent years of teaching spirituality. In email exchanges with my former student, she wrote in an Ignatian spirit about the gift of review, or the grace of returning to a previous prayer period, through which insights can be savored, deepened, and focused anew. As she put it: "Thank you for contacting me a few weeks ago. It's been a blessed few weeks. Through this exchange, I seem to have recovered from [a recent] spiritual downfall. I am currently [details of the ministry] and there had been such spiritual tiredness that I forgot that significant moment I had with Jesus. *Just remembering that moment for the past few weeks brought back my joy and hope being a child of God and I actually became free from some spiritual shackles that I had been carrying for ten years*. It is so mysterious how God works" (italics mine).

Several years after this initial experience of Ignatian group spiritual reading at Bethany Spirituality Center, one of my colleagues encouraged me to facilitate this form of prayer in a seminary class we would be teaching together.[35] I had felt comfortable doing so in another class I taught on contemplative listening, an introductory course in the art of spiritual direction. Due to the subject matter, enrollment in that particular class was limited to twenty students and group discussion (and group prayer) came more naturally. But my colleague and I were team-teaching a class of sixty students, and I did not know how to create a spirit of shared attentiveness to biblical narrative in a group of that size.

Despite having encountered the power of Ignatian meditation on class retreats with students, when I first led Ignatian meditation in a larger classroom context on campus I was surprised by the ways the scripture engaged students. The text for the day, Jesus calming the storm (Mk 4:35–41), allowed students to confront various kinds of pain, whether crushing disappointments long buried or anger at God long suppressed. Many identified with the disciples, furiously pouring water out of the boat and pleading with Jesus, "Don't you care that we are drowning?" Others spoke of a deep disbelief in Jesus's power, or in his compassion. Still others admitted to personal storms in their own lives and their yearning for calm in the midst of their studies or ministry and family demands. In one instance, the images returned to the student several months later, having been previously unresolved, and continued to invoke meaning and draw out fears. As the student now describes it:

Several years ago, during a classroom exercise of *lectio divina* and imaginative prayer based on Mark 4:35–41, I found myself visualizing the scene of Jesus and the disciples in the boat. As the scene became clear to my mind, I realized that I was one of the disciples. Soon, it was just Jesus and me in the boat. Jesus was sleeping in the bottom of the boat, and I was worried about the storm. The waves crashed around us, lightning lit up the sky, and the thunder shook the timbers of the boat. Suddenly, the image changed. Jesus was no longer sleeping. Now he was nailed to the mast. I understood that the mast was actually the Cross. I fled this image, and my time of prayer ended. I was very disturbed by this scene and could not understand what it meant.

A few months later, during another [classroom] session of *lectio divina*, on an unrelated passage, I found myself suddenly back in the scene from Mark 4. Everything was the same. It began as in the scripture. Then it shifted to Jesus, nailed to the mast. Although I was still disturbed, this time, instead of fleeing, I inquired about the meaning of the scene. And deep in my spirit, I came to an understanding. Jesus was nailed to the mast because I wanted him to be the sail for the boat. I wanted him to use his energies to get me out of my storm-tossed seas. But this desire was a tragedy. Because while God certainly does *not* desire us to be in pain, God *does* desire to be with us. And God desires to be with us in *all* of our life experiences—joys and sorrows. God had been trying to show me that it is possible to find peace and rest, even when life is difficult (and life will be difficult). But I

did not want to hear this message. Instead of resting
in God, spending time with God, even, perhaps especially, in the midst of the storm, I wanted to *use* God,
in order to flee life's difficulties.

This scene still haunts me, still challenges me. It
still pushes me to dwell with God when the storms
come.[36]

A final group of students experienced Jesus speaking peace
into their own lives through the text, whether as tender tran-
quility or an authoritative command, "Peace, be still!" And
with that encounter, anxieties carried into the classroom were
released. Whatever the students' engagement with the text—
a few indeed struggled to enter the scene at all; imaginative
prayer takes some patience and practice—the opportunity to
immerse oneself in the biblical scene opened up fresh honesty
in conversation with Christ and with each other by unmasking pain, doubt, and hidden hopes. Often, through these
experiences with the compassion of Christ, students have
written about receiving greater compassion for themselves,
their classmates, and even those in their lives they may have
struggled to love (or forgive) for long seasons of time. A genuine openness and a spirit of kindness enter the classroom
ethos, and a new kind of learning community is created

The Benedictine scholar Jean Leclercq writes beautifully
about the importance of biblical imagination in his seminal
work *The Love of Learning and the Desire for God:*

Another important factor explained by rumination
and reminiscence is the power of imagination of the
medieval [mindset] . . . this faculty . . . possesses a
vigor and a preciseness. . . . [The] imagination per-
mitted [readers of Scripture] to picture, to 'make

present,' to see beings with all the details provided by the texts: the colors and dimensions of things, the clothing, bearing, and actions of the people, the complex environment in which they move. [These readers of Scripture] liked to describe them and, so to speak, re-create them, giving very sharp relief to images and feelings. . . . The biblical words did not become trite; people never got used to them. Scripture, which they liked to compare to a river or a well, remained a fountain that was always fresh.[37]

And as my colleague Dennis Olson mentioned to our cohort group of advisees several years ago, "One third of the Old Testament is in poetry . . . so if we are going to be good readers of scripture, we need to learn how to read with imagination, metaphor, and creativity, because that is what poetry calls forth from its readers."[38] Yet many students of scripture have become hesitant to employ our imaginative faculties while exploring scripture; the right brain has become suspect in our approach to theology, and even our approach to God.[39] As Olson continued in his missive, "I thought the [use of the imagination] was wonderful as a way to loosen up some of the students and work with an alternative to the more linear, analytical and prosaic way in which academic study is often done."[40] And as J. R. R. Tolkien remarked to C. S. Lewis when Lewis struggled with the mystery of faith, "Your problem . . . is that your imagination isn't strong enough. When you read the great stories of literature or the fairy tales you love, you allow yourself to be swept up and swept away. But when you come to the stories of the Gospels, you become 'narrow and empiricist.' . . . Your imagination shuts down, and you start asking all kinds of rational questions you don't ask otherwise."

Chris Anderson elaborates on this crucial exchange in Lewis's life, where Lewis finally learned to steal past the "dragons" of reason: "We 'freeze' when we come to Scripture. . . . We feel restrained." But here's "the key, Tolkien says. The story of Christ should be seen as a story like those other stories, just as beautiful and powerful, and it should work on you in the same way, through your imagination and your heart. But with this difference: this story really happened."[41]

Conclusion

This chapter is a testament to the longing for compassion in all of our lives, and to the power of the classroom to release compassion and kindness from across multiple religious traditions. We yearn for a kinder world, for peace in our spirits and in our communities, and for the healing of profound brokenness both within and without. Mindfulness meditation practices, transcendental meditation, *lectio divina*, and Ignatian meditation (or spiritual reading) all contribute to the fulfillment of this longing in our lives.[42]

Although this book is written for scholars and teachers in both Western and Eastern religious traditions, I have focused this particular chapter on my experience of Jesus the Christ through Ignatian contemplation. One reason for my unabashed exploration of Ignatian—and thus Christian—meditation in this chapter arises from that first experience of Buddhist compassion meditation at the American Academy of Religion conference, described at the start of this chapter.[43] Love poured in from an unexpected fountain, and it serves no one for me to hide that source, even out of seeming respect or deference for other traditions. I am deeply indebted to my colleagues from Buddhist, Hindu, and Taoist traditions for helping me embrace the merit of slowing down in the class-room, and especially to colleagues who have introduced me to compassion meditations.[44] At the same time, I don't want to neglect resources from my own tradition, or let those living wells of Christian prayer become stagnant; for they too can inspire more compassion in the world."[45]

Notes

1. The Contemplative Studies Group is now referred to as the Con-templative Studies Program Unit within the American Academy of Religion.

2. Despite formal academic training in Buddhism during my undergradu-ate years, I had not before this AAR conference almost ten years ago practiced meditation with Buddhist practitioners. My Buddhism pro-fessors in the Religious Studies Department at Yale University were themselves devoted practitioners, even hinting that they hoped for us to become Buddhist alongside them, but they dared not invite us to meditate during class time. And though I had Buddhist friends from my high school days onward, I did not experience meditation until this colleague invited us into his spiritual practice. That this was accept-able at an academic conference represents a shift in the value of practice even in scholarly settings (though this seems to be more acceptable in many sectors for Eastern religious practices than Christian ones).

3. See the introduction to the book in which this chapter was originally published, *The Soul of Higher Education: Contemplative Pedagogy, Research and Institutional Life for the Twenty-First Century*, for fur-ther background on the inspiration for the volume. While my coedi-tor, Margaret Benefiel, and I have benefited tremendously from our participation in the Contemplative Studies Program Unit, we also observed that it has weighed more heavily in presenting perspectives from Eastern religious traditions, an observation that Louis Komjathy makes poignantly about the field in general in *Introducing Contempla-tive Studies* (Hoboken, NJ: Blackwell, 2017). Through that volume we desire to make more space for voices from the Christian tradition alongside other wisdom streams.

4. Of that "moment in his forties when the image of the Great Lion first occurred to him," Lewis explains, "I think I had been having a good many dreams of lions about that time. Apart from that, I don't know where the Lion came from or why He came. But once He was there He pulled the whole story together, and soon He pulled the six other Narnia stories in after Him." C. S. Lewis, *Of Other Worlds—Essays and Stories,* ed. Walter Hooper (New York: Harcourt, Brace & World, 1966), 42.

5. Mary Rose O'Reilley, *The Peaceable Classroom* (Portsmouth, NH: Heinemann, 1993), x. As the back jacket of O'Reilley's book explains, "When a professor dropped this question into a colloquium for young college teachers in 1967, at the height of the Vietnam War, most people shuffled their feet. For Mary Rose O'Reilley it was a question that would not go away; *The Peaceable Classroom* records one attempt to answer it. Out of her own experience, primarily as a college English teacher, she writes about certain moral connections between school and the outside world, making clear that the kind of environment created in the classroom determines a whole series of choices students make in the future, especially about issues of peace and justice."

6. There are, of course, a variety of meditation practices within each religious tradition (e.g., apophatic and cataphatic), but for the purposes of this chapter, I focus on one form that employs the use of images (rather than seeking to empty one's meditation of words and images) as a unique source of access to divine compassion. In response to my sending this chapter to him, Tilden Edwards wrote: "I have used a guided meditation a number of times that . . . seems to connect with what you describe. It involves the story of the blind beggar Bartimaeus, who leaps up to come to Jesus as he passes by (Mk 10:46). I read the story to a group (after a little settling breath prayer), then invite the listeners to enter the scene with all their senses; eventually I ask them to let the scene fade, except for Jesus. You are alone with him, face to face. Open yourself to whatever may spontaneously happen (such as asking him a question, saying something to him, seeing what he says or does). Then after some minutes I ask them to let every image fade, and be in an open, wordless, imageless, spacious, receptive presence for a few minutes (or some such words). When I did that in an Episcopal church once, the rector afterward (he was about fifty years old or so) told me

that he experienced Jesus for the first time in his life! You'll note that in my guidance I began with a cataphatic practice, and then let the person rest in an apophatic presence, seeing the two as complementary." Tilden Edwards, personal email communication, July 29, 2018.

7. See the entry *compassio* in Albert Blaise, *Dictionnaire Latin-Français des auteurs chrétiens* (Turnhout: Brepols, 1954), 180. See also Oliver Davies, *A Theology of Compassion* (Grand Rapids, MI: Eerdmans, 2003) for the most recent systematic treatment of compassion. As Bernard McGinn notes in his recent lectures, "The Compassion of the Mystics," at the Gerald May Seminar of the Shalem Institute of Spiritual Formation (November 9–10, 2018), "Compassion involves an affective sharing in the feeling of the other person, an entering into another's subjectivity," according to Davies, *A Theology of Compassion* (London: SCM Press, 2001), 232–33. McGinn further explains, "God's 'loving kindness' (*hesed*) towards his people is often linked with the terms *rahum* and *raham*, often translated as compassion, that are cognate with the word for womb (*rehem*). . . . In the New Testament a similar somatic emphasis pervades the major term used for compassion, the Greek *splagkna*, literally 'guts, innards, bowels.'" Helmut Köster, "*Splagknon, splagknizomai ktl*," *Theological Dictionary of the New Testament* ed. Gerhard Kittel (Grand Rapids: Eerdmans, 1964), 7:548–59. See also Martha Nussbaum, "Compassion: The Basic Social Emotion," *Social Philosophy and Policy* 13, no. 1 (Winter 1996): 27–58; Monica Hellwig, *Jesus, the Compassion of God* (Wilmington, DE: Glazier, 1983); Michael Downey, "Compassion," in *The New Dictionary of Catholic Spirituality*, ed. Michael Downey (Collegeville: Liturgical Press, 1993), 192–93; and Janet Ruffing, "God's Compassionate Heart—the Source of Compassionate Accompaniment," *Studies in Spirituality* 23 (2013): 201–11; "'They Say We Are Wound with Mercy Round and Round': The Mystical Ground of Compassion," *Studies in Spirituality* 26 (2016): 33–44.

8. Fyodor Dostoevsky, *The Grand Inquisitor: with Related Chapters from The Brothers Karamazov,* ed. Charles Guignon (Indianapolis: Hackett Publishing, 1993), 7–8.

9. This "advanced training workshop" was sponsored by the Volunteers of America, the Braxton Institute, and the Soul Repair Center at Brite

Divinity School, and was held at Trinity Episcopal Church in Princeton, New Jersey, September 9–12, 2017.

10. One of the workshop leaders with whom I spoke has written a bit about her story in Rita Nakashima Brock and Rebecca Ann Parker, *Proverbs of Ashes: Violence, Redemptive Suffering, and the Search for What Saves Us* (Boston: Beacon Press, 2002). See esp. pp. 209–10 for the power of the imagination in counseling sessions, to illumine light, hope, and healing.

11. See, for example, Brock and Parker, *Proverbs of Ashes*. I was struck in my conversations with Rebecca Parker by the depth of her kindness, which seemed to me related to her own experience of trauma and subsequent healing. In fact, when I asked about the sources of her compassion, she explained that her own suffering created a greater capacity for compassion in her life. Other speakers responded similarly when I asked them directly how they cultivate (or have cultivated) compassion in their lives; they concluded through this query that their own experience of suffering made them gracious toward others—and likely that which brought them into helping professions in the first place. It is important to note, however, that not all experiences of trauma or suffering lead automatically to greater compassion for others; pain can break or destroy the human spirit. In the words of Richard Rohr, "If we do not transform our pain, we will most assuredly transmit it. If we cannot find a way to make our wounds into sacred wounds, we invariably give up on life and humanity." Richard Rohr, "Transforming Our Pain," Center for Action and Contemplation, February 26, 2016, https:// cac.org/transforming-our-pain-2016-02-26. The Ignatian pathway is one valuable means by which our pain can be transformed into compassionate solidarity with others.

12. Quoted in James Cone, "Theology's Great Sin: Silence in the Face of White Supremacy," *Union Seminary Quarterly Review* 55, no. 3–4 (2001): 1–14; emphasis mine. Cone adds, "There are few Whites who really know how to express that sort of solidarity."

13. In Albert J. Raboteau, *American Prophets: Seven Religious Radicals and Their Struggle for Social and Political Justice* (Princeton, NJ: Princeton University Press, 2016), 117; emphasis mine.

14. This was also an important theme for conversation at the New Contemplative Leaders Exchange at St. Benedict's Monastery in Snowmass, Colorado.

15. Henri Nouwen, *The Way of the Heart* (New York: Random House Publishing, 2003), 15–25. Nouwen adds, "Solitude is the place of the great struggle and the great encounter—the struggle against the compulsions of the false self, and the encounter with the God who offers himself as the substance of the new self." He continues, "Our primary task in solitude is not to pay undue attention to the many faces which assail us, but to keep the eyes of our mind and heart on him who is our divine savior. Only in the context of grace can we face our sin; only in the place of healing do *we dare to show our wounds; only with a single-minded attention to Christ can we give up our clinging fears and face our own true nature. As we come to realize that it is not we who live, but Christ who lives in us, that he is our true self, we can slowly let our compulsions melt away and begin to experience the freedom of the children of God. And then we can look back with a smile and realize that we aren't even angry or greedy anymore.* . . . Solitude is thus the place of purification and transformation, the place of the great struggle and the great encounter. . . . It is the place where Christ remodels us in his own image and frees us from the victimizing compulsions of the world."

16. Gregory Boyle, "Lessons from the Field: Kinship as an Intervention" (lecture, Princeton University, February 22, 2017). I give thanks to my student Jennifer Lewis, and my ministry colleague BJ Katen-Narvell, for relaying this exchange to me.

17. See also Beverly J. Lanzetta, "Wound of Love: Feminine *Theosis* and Embodied Mysticism in Teresa of Avila," in *The Participatory Turn: Spirituality, Mysticism, Religious Studies,* ed. Jorge N. Ferrer and Jacob H. Sherman (New York: SUNY Press: 2008), esp. 228–230, for Teresa of Avila's understanding of solidarity with Christ in his suffering compassion for the world.

18. Henri Nouwen, Donald McNeill, and Douglas Morrison, *Compassion: A Reflection on the Christian Life* (London: Darton, Longman and Todd, 2008), 108. Earlier in the same passage, he writes, "One of the most powerful experiences in a life of compassion is the expansion of our hearts into a world-embracing space of healing from which no one

is excluded. Prayer for others, therefore, cannot be seen as an extraordinary exercise that must be practiced from time to time. Rather, it is the very beat of a compassionate heart. To pray for a friend who is ill, for a student who is depressed, for a teacher who is in conflict; for people in prisons, in hospitals, on battlefields; for those who are victims of injustice, who are hungry, poor, without shelter; for those who risk their career, their health, and even their life in struggle for social justice; for leaders of church and state to pray for all these people is not a futile effort to influence God's will, but a hospitable gesture by which we invite our neighbors into the center of our hearts" (p. 107). Later, he continues, "When we come before God with the needs of the world, the healing love of the Holy Spirit that touches us, touches with the same power all those whom we bring before [God]. Compassionate prayer does not encourage the self-serving individualism that leads us to flee from people or to fight them. On the contrary, by deepening our awareness of our common suffering, prayer draws us closer together in the presence of the Holy Spirit" (p. 110).

19. At the same time, note the important distinction between primary and secondary suffering, or between the suffering of the victim and that of the witness. Weingarten, for example, wants to "ensure that at no point do we ever confuse whatever suffering might come from witnessing with the suffering that we are witnessing." They "are not akin to each other," and we "have an ethical responsibility to ensure that we are not confused by this." David Denborough, "Trauma, Meaning, Witnessing and Action: An Interview with Kaethe Weingarten," *International Journal of Narrative and Community Work*, nos 3–4 (2005): 72–76.

20. Nicholas Wolterstorff, *Lament for a Son* (Grand Rapids, MI: Wm B. Eerdmans, 1987), 81–82.

21. In some circles, Ignatian prayer has been considered less "contemplative" because of its generally cataphatic nature (since many Christian contemplatives have focused on apophatic prayer). See n. 6 above.

22. For example, the actor Andrew Garfield, raised in a nonreligious home, confesses to "falling in love" with this Jesus as he went through these exercises in preparation for his role in the film *Silence*. Brendan Busse, "Andrew Garfield Played a Jesuit in Silence, But He Didn't Expect to Fall in Love with Jesus," *America*, January 23,

2017, https://www.americamagazine.org/arts-culture/2017/01/10/andrew-garfield-played-jesuit-silence-he-didnt-expect-fall-love-jesus.

23. Henri Nouwen, *The Return of the Prodigal Son: A Story of Homecoming* (New York: Image, 1994), 12–14, 62–64.

24. For a brief biography of Ignatius's life, see Elizabeth Liebert, "Ignatius of Loyola (1491–1556), *The Spiritual Exercises,*" in Arthur Holder, ed., *Christian Spirituality: The Classics* (London: Routledge, 2009); James Martin, "A Way of Proceeding: What Is Ignatian Spirituality?" in *A Jesuit Guide to (Almost) Everything: A Spirituality for Real Life* (San Francisco: HarperOne, 2010); or Margaret Silf, "Meet Your Guide: St. Ignatius Loyola," in *Inner Compass* (Chicago: Loyola Press, 2007).

25. Hence the motto of the Jesuits: "A.M.D.G."—*Ad Maiorem Dei Gloriam* ("for the greater glory of God").

26. Michael Harter, *Hearts on Fire: Praying with Jesuits* (Chicago: Loyola Press, 2012).

27. James Martin, *A Jesuit Guide to (Almost) Everything: A Spirituality for Real Life* (San Francisco: HarperOne, 2010), 17.

28. See Barbara Newman's essay, "The Contemplative Classroom," in *The Soul of Higher Education*, ed. Margaret Benefiel and Bo Karen Lee (Charlotte, NC: Information Age Publishing, 2019). See also Elizabeth Liebert, "Ignatius of Loyola (1491–1556), *The Spiritual Exercises,*" in Arthur Holder, ed., *Christian Spirituality: The Classics* (London: Routledge, 2009) for the surprisingly wide circulation of *The Spiritual Exercises* in interdenominational ministries of spiritual direction, community Bible studies, church small groups, etc.

29. Interestingly, in his expositions in *The Life of Christ*, Ludolph of Saxony himself uses this approach of cultivating the senses through this kind of imaginative reading of scripture passages.

30. See Brendan Busse, "Grace Enough: Andrew Garfield on the Ignatian Journey that Led Him Through 'Silence,'" *America* 216, no. 2 (January 23, 2017): 42–49, in which the actor Andrew Garfield relates Ignatian meditation to the craft of acting and filmmaking.

31. For more details on the four weeks, see Elizabeth Liebert, "Ignatius of Loyola (1491–1556), *The Spiritual Exercises,*" in Arthur Holder, ed., *Christian Spirituality: The Classics* (London: Routledge, 2009); and

Kevin O'Brien, *The Ignatian Adventure: Experiencing the Spiritual Exercises of St. Ignatius in Daily Life* (Chicago: Loyola Press, 2011).

32. This form of prayer goes by various names, such as "Gospel contemplation" (James Martin, *A Jesuit Guide to (Almost) Everything* [San Francisco: HarperOne, 2010], 145–162); and "composition of place" or "imaginative prayer" (Margaret Silf, *Inner Compass: An Invitation to Ignatian Spirituality* [Chicago: Loyola Press, 2007], 12–24).

33. For one example of guided meditations, see the app "Pray As You Go" (or website Pray As You Go, https://pray-as-you-go.org); the meditation dated Sunday 9/30/18 is particularly helpful in experiencing "Gospel contemplation" or "composition of place."

34. I give thanks to my former student for permission to include her experience, dated October 2008. In our email exchanges, as we clarified details of memory, she wrote, "The thing that struck me the most was how smooth and clear that encounter was. It was as if I was originally there in that scene and Jesus was standing in front of me. He *was* God ... but ... he just looked at me in a very warm and loving way ... I never before experienced prayer so sweet.... For me, this experience was life changing. It was like seeing heaven."

35. Thanks go to Richard Osmer for encouraging this experiment in our classroom. See Bo Karen Lee, "The 'Double-Pointed Ellipse': Integrating Spirituality and Mission," in *Consensus and Conflict: Practical Theology for Congregations in the Work of Richard R. Osmer*, ed. Kenda Dean, Amanda Drury, Andrew Root, and Blair Bertrand (Eugene, OR: Wipf and Stock, 2019), 92–104. A few of the examples in this chapter are featured also in that essay. Thanks to Wipf and Stock for permission to reprint a few pages from that essay in this chapter.

36. I give thanks to this class member for permission to reprint this narrative and for their generosity in sending it to me, even six years afterward.

37. Jean Leclerq, *The Love of Learning and the Desire for God: A Study of Monastic Culture* (New York: Fordham University Press, 1982), 75.

38. Dennis Olson, email messages to author, November 6–7, 2013. The exchange revolved around the use of the visual arts in *lectio divina* during a cohort group gathering. In his words, "The visual arts have always been an important stimulus and aid to faith in the Christian

tradition." Thanks to Dennis Olson for permission to quote from his emails in this essay.

39. Even the late Fr. Kevin Seasoltz, OSB, of St. John's University mentioned lovingly to me that as a more left-brained monk, he is more comfortable with exegesis and rational meditation, which he learned well from *lectio divina* and his Benedictine tradition; he admitted to me that this kind of Ignatian imagination eludes his realm of experience. (Admittedly, Jean Leclercq champions Benedictine imagination in *lectio divina*, so this unfamiliarity with imaginative contemplation is not inherently Benedictine.) At the close of our conversation, Fr. Kevin encouraged me to write a piece on Ignatian forms of imaginative prayer (so that he could read and benefit from it). This chapter is dedicated, in part, to his memory.

40. See n. 36 above.

41. Chris Anderson, *Light When It Comes: Trusting Joy, Facing Darkness & Seeing God in Everything* (Grand Rapids, MI: Eerdmans, 2016), 33; cf. *The Letters of C. S. Lewis to Arthur Greeves,* ed. Walter Hooper (New York: Macmillan, 1979), 193.

42. See chapters 2, 7, 12, 14 in *The Soul of Higher Education: Contemplative Pedagogy, Research and Institutional Life for the Twenty-First Century,* ed. Margaret Benefiel and Bo Karen Lee (Charlotte, NC: Information Age Publishing, 2019) for these various kinds of meditation in the classroom. See also David Kahane, "Learning about Obligation, Compassion and Global Justice: The Place of Contemplative Pedagogy," in *Contemplative Learning and Inquiry Across Disciplines*, ed. Olen Gunnlaugson et al. (Albany: State University of New York Press, 2014), 119–132, for an excellent treatment of the relationship between classroom meditation practices and social justice sensitivities in our students. A recurring image for me comes from Revelation 22:1–2: "Then the angel showed me the river of the water of life, bright as crystal, flowing from the throne of God. . . . On either side of the river is the tree of life with its twelve kinds of fruit, producing its fruit each month; and the leaves of the tree are for the healing of the nations."

43. Thanks go to Belden Lane, who convinced me in his essay, "Writing in Spirituality As a Self-Implicating Act: Reflections on Authorial

Disclosure and the Hiddenness of the Self," in *Exploring Christian spirituality: Essays in Honor of Sandra M. Schneiders*, ed. Bruce H. Lescher and Elizabeth Liebert (Mahwah, NJ: Paulist Press, 2006) that authorial self-disclosure can be a gift to the reader rather than an obstacle. The objective and hidden authorial voice is indeed a myth, he argues, and I am now a believer in this point of view (after years of training otherwise).

44. I thank especially Daniel Barbezat, Rhonda Magee, and Mirabai Bush, whose workshops at various Contemplative Pedagogies conferences revolutionized my thinking about what could be possible in classroom spaces.

45. During one particular conference of the Association for Contemplative Mind in Higher Education, it became evident that most of the scholars came from an Eastern perspective, and that many of the speakers had deep suspicions of Christianity (and for good reason). Though I remained very sympathetic to their aversion to Christianity, I personally grieved the absence of Christ from the conversation. As I described to my colleague Margaret Benefiel, I felt heartbroken in some ways— because it seemed my lover was left outside the door and unwelcomed. This experience was part of the inspiration for our book *The Soul of Higher Education: Contemplative Pedagogy, Research and Institutional Life for the Twenty-first Century* (Charlottle, NC: Information Age Publishing, 2019), in which this chapter originally appears. See the Introduction to that volume (pp. x–xi) for further details.

Ignatian forms of imaginative meditation also infuse my class preparation times, as well as planning meetings with my teaching team. When I meet with teaching assistants, for example, I often invite them into three or four minutes of silent meditation before we begin our active planning for the semester. I ask them to imagine our students, the classroom space, and God's presence among us. What hopes emerge for our students and for ourselves as teachers? The desires that emerge from this brief time of listening and quiet imagination often shape the core of our syllabus and create a spirit of shared ownership and joyful possibility for the class.

EMBODIMENT, COMPASSION, AND HEALING

Contemplation in the Bible: Where, When, How?

MARK LONGHURST

"If all human beings were lovers, the distinction between mysticism and non-mysticism would disappear."[1]

—Novalis

On the surface, my life is not very contemplative. I pastor a small church in the Berkshires of Massachusetts, working to develop a ministry of social justice, spiritual transformation, and the arts. My wife and I parent two wonderful and rowdy young boys. We are embedded in a local community, often bring work home at night, and the morning routine to usher the boys to school each day is nearly always frenzied. My attempt to do a Centering Prayer sit before the boys wake up typically is interrupted by the pitter-patter of boys waking up. I am anxious and impatient more than I care to admit.

What gives me encouragement, though, is that the treasures of the contemplative tradition are now available to everyone. The living stream of Christian mysticism flows where it will. While contemplation throughout the Christian tradition has typically been associated with silence, prayer-filled scripture reading and solitude, monasteries, while critical bearers of the tradition, no longer have a corner on the market. As access to the mystical tradition expands, so must the definitions of contemplation expand.

To put it directly, maybe I can be a mystic too—or at least an ordinary one.

A more seismic shift in spiritual paradigms is underway, though, than simply my own ability to pursue the once-obscure mystical path. After all, with the right resources, white, middle-class, heterosexual men like me can shop the spiritual marketplace for as many self-improvement schemes as we wish. What's at stake is not only *who* can contemplate God but also the places, times, and means of contemplation.

The Bible is a primary site for Christian contemplative awakening. It's the text monks and nuns have chewed on for centuries in their quest for loving union with God. Early Desert Fathers and Mothers followed ancient Israel's practice of chanting the psalms. The founder of Western monasticism, Benedict of Nursia, institutionalized psalm-singing through scheduled prayer times called the Divine Office. Origen of Alexandria launched a tradition of mystical commentary on the Bible, first suggesting that the erotic Song of Songs symbolizes God's relationship to the soul. Gregory of Nyssa and Pseudo-Dionysius saw Moses's ascent to Mount Sinai as a paradigmatic moment of the soul encountering divine darkness.

It's well worth wondering, though, just what sort of contemplation in which the biblical characters themselves are engaged. Monks, nuns, and Spirit-attuned theologians pioneered the practice of contemplation *through* the biblical text, but what might contemplation *in* the biblical text itself look like on its own terms?

Generations of historical critical scholars have helped Bible readers recover an awareness of context, original languages, and literary art form. These are developments to be welcomed rather than shunned. To paraphrase one particularly keen Bible reader, the author and former pastor Rob Bell, "We don't read the Bible literally. We read it literately."[2] But as critically informed readers ruminate on scriptural texts today, what emerges instead is distinctly not contemplative by the traditional Western Christian standards of silence, stillness, and solitude.

Maybe this is as it should be.

Sure, Elijah encounters God in a still small voice, or, as 1 Kings puts it, "a sound of sheer silence" (19:12). But the Hebrew Bible's Yahweh is known as much for speech and noise as revelation through silence. The Oxford historian Diarmaid MacCulloch surveys biblical silence and reminds us that it's Yahweh who causes earth to reel and rock in 2 Samuel 22:8 and speaks creation into existence.[3] "Let there be light," this God says, and there is.

To consider the Bible's characters experiencing contemplation, a reorientation of definitions is in order.

Or maybe the Bible's flawed and all-too-human characters can be mystics too?

Maybe the Bible's visions of contemplation will help expand what contemplation can be in our own time?

What if living under Empire, as nearly all the biblical characters do, shapes contemplation in startling ways?[4]

What if, as theologian Barbara A. Holmes claims, the world itself is the cloister of the contemplative?[5]

What follows in this chapter, then, are three stops along a way of uncovering contemplation in the Bible. The first stop asks *where* people in the Bible contemplate. With the book of Exodus as a guide, the journey involves encountering God in deserts and mountains, both archetypal and literal. Through the prophet Jeremiah's mystical-prophetic witness, the second stop observes that *when* people contemplate God in the Bible it is usually in a time of Empire and often involves tears. John's gospel inspires the third stop by detailing *how* people contemplate God through abiding in the presence and love of Christ.

Contemplating God in Deserts and Mountains

I'm no desert dweller. I happen to love New Mexico's dry dirt, short trees, and adobe houses, but I wouldn't dare journey for days in the actual desert. When my wife and I first discussed moving to western Massachusetts, I asked, "Is there an independent movie theater? Where's the nearest craft brewery?"

The desert, however, is a rich and longstanding image in the Jewish and Christian traditions.[6] Ancient Christian monks wandered to the most remote and craggy outposts they could find and set up camp. The barren landscape became a spiritual metaphor for the interior purification or "letting go" process needed to meet God.

The ancient Israelites are a wilderness, nomadic people. They contemplate God in deserts and on mountaintops, on the margins and on the move. Of course, the image of the promised land looms large in the Jewish imagination, but the desert persistently haunts the people as symbol and harsh reality.

It's the wilderness—in Hebrew the same word for desert, *midbar*[7]—that wields transformative, liberating power. The dramatic, mountain-quaking revelation at Sinai that Moses experiences is preceded first by the people's escape from Egyptian slavery and time spent wandering in the desert. But before Moses leads the people in the archetypal freedom flight from Empire, he himself goes out to the desert.

He has fled Egypt, having murdered an Egyptian, and taken refuge in a land called Midian. One day, Moses is keeping the flocks of his father-in-law, Jethro (Exodus 3:1). He leads his flock into the wilderness-desert and arrives at a mountain, where he stumbles across a burning bush and receives Yahweh's liberating call.

His leadership is galvanized by his own divine desert encounter.

Before the people arrive at Sinai, they too trek through the desert. But the desert is tough and impersonal. It does not care about people. It has its own identity and will. It does not bend easily to our desires, if at all. The desert is not only a stop on the way to the mountain or an unfortunate detour on the way to the promised land but also a destination itself.

The Israelites learn this lesson with great complaint. They cross the Red Sea, fleeing Pharaoh's chariots while divine power holds waves at bay. Once in the wilderness-desert, the people face hunger, thirst, and armed enemies. Newly liberated, they nevertheless romanticize their oppression. They start to pine for Egypt's full meals. They become thirsty. They protest Moses's leadership. "Why did you bring us out into the desert, to kill us?" they ask (Exodus 16:3). God sends food from heaven for sustenance. God gives water that flows out of a rock. They run into other desert nomads, called Amalek, and are forced to fight to protect themselves.

The desert is the in-between space of testing, divine revelation, and transformation. It's the job loss and search, the dissolution of a marriage, the grief after a beloved's death. It's also the place to discover God's freedom and presence, from which a voice cries out, "Prepare the way of the Lord" (Mark 1:3). The story of Israel in the desert is also the story of the gospels, the way retread by Jesus. Once baptized and immersed in water, Jesus, too, is thrust into the wilderness-desert. Moses lingers at Mount Sinai for forty days and forty nights while, generations later, Jesus endures the desert and Satan's cross examination for forty days and forty nights.[8]

Once tested and proven true in the desert, Jesus *returns* to the desert. It's as if Jesus chooses the uncertain liminality of desert to frame his life. Mark's gospel includes rich, brief lines that suggest Jesus's dedication to contemplation. They often simply read, "Jesus withdrew to a quiet place." Writers on silent prayer have often turned to these verses in the hopes that Jesus, too, values silence. But Jesus's embrace of silence is tied to landscape: the Greek word *eremos* means both a solitary *and* desert place (see Mark 6:31).[9] When Jesus goes off to pray, he is not only stealing solitude, he is going to the desert.

The desert is the archetypal and literal place where we meet God, the place of fierce love. Deserts of loss, grief, pain and literal sand strip down our pretensions, as if to say that preparing for God's way requires abandonment of all our prior ways. The ways that we are in the world are all-too-often directed from addiction and a desire for more. The desert demands us to be emptied rather than filled, to show up and be tested, for divine fire to refine our desire, to face inner barrenness head-on, just as Jesus faces down the devil in the wilderness.

We are confronted with our naked self in the desert. There's no place for our pride, lust, anger, resentment, or need for approval to hide. No amount of posturing will shield us from the desert sun's unremitting glare. Its clarity may even stir us to long once again for the seemingly safe oppression of Egypt.

Or the truth that the desert peels away may cause us to plunge headlong in love with God, to say with the poet of the Song of Songs, "Who is that coming up from the wilderness, leaning upon her beloved?" (8:5)

Contemplation as Prophetic Lament Under Empire

Exploring the contours of biblical contemplation is danger-ous. It upsets comfortable worldviews, forces us to see real-ity and ourselves as we are, and demands nothing less than whole-life transformation. This is nowhere the case more than with the Hebrew prophets and in particular the prophet Jeremiah.

Jeremiah is a mystic with God's Word burning in his bones. He's one of those prophets whose language is so extreme, violent, and offensive that it is often excruciating to read. He is R-rated, holds nothing back, spares no metaphor. He wields his broken, bloody heart, which mirrors God's bro-ken, bloody heart, for all to see. He functions as a literary poet that we know is great but whose work resides on our shelf collecting dust. We might place his disaster-ridden scroll alongside the medieval Italian poet Dante Alighieri's visions of hell and the contemporary American poet Charles Bukowski's drunken pulp.

Dire times, however, call for dire poetic and prophetic imaginations.

Ancient Israel in Jeremiah's day is at its end. The Assyrians have already conquered the north. Southern Israel, known as Judah, has survived over the years by the skin of its teeth. They have eked out an existence through realpolitik negotia-tion and pinball-like protection from whichever superpower happens to be ascendant in the moment: first Assyria, then briefly Egypt, until yet another Empire appears on the hori-zon. Encroaching from the East are the Babylonians, a rival power rising up to conquer the conquerors.[10]

Jeremiah steps into this breach, sees and names the writing on Israel's wall: it is over.

There is no escaping defeat. Jerusalem's ramparts are no match for Empire's chariots, soldiers, and swords. Israel is a puny nation sandwiched between greater powers; they are not the Babylonians main threat, of course, but they stand in the way. It's time, then, for Jeremiah and Israel to accept the unbearable burden of reality. It's time to realize that the oncoming war will destroy sacred places and objects, that cultures will be decimated, that people will be deported, and that innocents will die.

This is what Empire does, and this is what Empire will do.

God picks the prophet Jeremiah as a communications secretary and throws him into the political mess. In chapter 1, he receives a call, similar to Moses's call from God, to be a deliverer. Like Moses, he questions his fitness for duty. He says, "Truly I do not know how to speak, for I am only a boy" (1:6). The call functions similarly to other prophetic calls in the Hebrew Bible, except this time, instead of delivering the people *from* slavery as Moses did, Jeremiah announces God's intention to deliver the people *into* the hands of their oppressor. Sometimes God's messengers do not have good news to share.

Or, as a mentor used to say to me, the gospel is bad news before it is good.

Prophets are the Bible's public mystics. Prophet-mystics do not receive God's fiery word for their own personal edification; instead, they function as messengers of God's Word of justice and mercy to the people and king. Prophets are often in fundamental tension with kings. They dwell, as the Franciscan teacher Richard Rohr describes, on the edge of the inside.[11]

Jeremiah, on the one hand, firmly dwells on the edge. He is a pastor's kid from an insignificant village called Anathoth (1:1) He carries with him the typical ancient Israelite villager experience of crushing poverty, Assyrian overtaxation, and urban economic complicity with Empire at the expense of the rural poor.[12]

Outsider that he is, Jeremiah nevertheless has inside access. He maintains several friends in Jerusalem's high places: an elite scribe named Baruch, for one (chapter 45); a prominent man and family named Shaphon, for another (26:24). Jeremiah is a confidante and thorn in the side to kings, and, as disturbing as his poetry is, people listen to him.

In America's Trump-era of mainline church decline and evangelical soul-selling, contemporary equivalents to the prophet's role are rare. Ancient Israel built the faithful moral voice into their political structure. The prophet cries out on behalf of Yahweh for justice and the needs of the poor, holding the powerful accountable when they make a mockery of God's vision of wholeness: "For scoundrels are found among my people . . . they know no limits in deeds of wickedness" (5:26, 28). Wicked deeds, of course, span millennia. Were he to prophesy today, Jeremiah might level his ire at voter suppression or the denial and suppression of science.

The best American equivalent to the ancient prophet is likely Dr. Martin Luther King Jr. King could phone Lyndon B. Johnson on the same day that he went to jail for nonviolent civil disobedience protesting racial inequality. Like King, Jeremiah balanced both access and critical distance.

There are other prophets at the center in Jeremiah's day and ours, but these are, he tells us, false prophets. They are yes-men and -women who only tell of perpetual good news. Jeremiah rails against them: "They have treated the wound of my people carelessly, saying 'Peace, peace,' when there is no peace" (6:13–14).

They have treated the wound of my people carelessly.

Jeremiah's task is to display the wound in order to treat it. It is the same task as that of Bryan Stevenson, the founder of the Equal Justice Initiative and the force behind the new museum in Montgomery, Alabama, dedicated to the victims of lynching.[13] At this new museum, eight hundred large steel columns hang, each of them representing an American county and bearing the names, if known, of those murdered. To quote the *New York Times*, there hangs the name of Park Banks, "lynched in Mississippi in 1922 for carrying a photograph of a white woman." There hangs the name of "Caleb Gadly, hanged in Kentucky in 1894 for walking behind the wife of his white employer."

We carry such trauma and wounds in our collective hearts and bodies. There is no escape from the wound, no possibility of healing unless we first expose it.

Mystics are those, some say, who are one with God. Divine union is the end point of the classic mystical itinerary in the Christian tradition.[14] But the popular misconception of such language is that divine union is a stage enjoyed apart from the everyday, or worse yet, disconnected from the darkness, carelessly treating the wound or avoiding the wound altogether. There's a phrase for that in spirituality circles since the 1980s—*spiritual bypassing*—and it occurs when we use religion to overlook or cloak our emotional and psychological needs.[15]

Jeremiah does not fall into this trap. Jeremiah is a mystic gifted instead with Yahweh's terrifying words in his mouth and the holiness of tears. He *is* one with God, but the oneness is lament rather than repose.

The great Jewish writer Abraham Joshua Heschel even suggests that God's very self is grieving through Jeremiah. He writes that "Jeremiah depicted the dramatic tension of the inner life of God. [His] words are aglow with the divine pathos that can be reflected, but not pronounced: God is mourning Himself."[16] Jeremiah's heart has fallen in loving union with Yahweh to such a degree that there is no clear line where Jeremiah's heartbreak and Yahweh's sorrow begin.

Contemplation as Abiding in the Christ Vine

Thankfully, the Bible's trajectory of union with God is not all prophetic torment and grief. It is also mutual abiding-in-love. This is where John's gospel, the crown jewel of contemplation in the Bible, comes in. At the mystical heart of John's gospel is a message of divine indwelling or "abiding."

We abide in God and God abides in us.

As Jesus puts it to his disciples at their Last Supper together: "I am the vine, you are the branches. Those who abide in me and I in them bear much fruit, because apart from me you can do nothing" (Jn 15:5). Jesus and friends drink wine and eat bread while he takes the dinner conversation to a metaphysical level. He tells them that they are connected, one, growing together through and in love.

It's not the first time that readers have encountered the vine and her fruit in John's gospel. The symbol of Jesus as vine reaches back to Cana's wedding, to Jesus's first sign of turning water into wine. It's a memorable ministry launch. As the biblical scholar Allen Dwight Callahan puts it, "Jesus saves the wedding party from social disaster in a feat of miraculous sacrilege by turning consecrated vessels into an open bar."[17] He reminds wedding revelers that God's joyful and abundant life of the ages starts always today, not only later, and not only at temple, synagogue, or church.

Mystics are those who abide in God's relational flow of love. Mystics do not have to be extraordinary people; mystics are, instead, those who go beyond themselves to abide in love's flow of giving and receiving. This going beyond the self can take place on dramatic mountain heights, as Moses did, but more likely it happens through the mundane inner choices we make while, say, doing the laundry or handling disagreements with our spouse.

We all can be ordinary mystics, but I've heard many either ignore or write off mystics as passive do-nothing, good-for-nothing navel-gazers. Or, more subtly, we may treat mystics as spiritual heroes of the faith, whose pinnacles of relationship with God we can never hope to attain.

Mystics are my heroes, but not in the unapproachable sense. Rather, mystics remind us of the heart's spiritual potency to love. As the poet-writer Novalis says, "If all human beings were lovers, the distinction between mysticism and non-mysticism would disappear."[18]

Yet John knows well that there's a long Jewish heritage of calling Israel herself the vine. With astonishing confidence, and as a Jew, Jesus calls himself the vine. For prophets such as Jeremiah, vines symbolized Israel, usually wayward and fruitless, having disobeyed Torah, and worshipped false gods of security and status rather than Yahweh. God laments Israel's spiritual fate by visions of grapes gone wrong: "Yet I planted you as a choice vine, from the purest stock. How then did you turn degenerate and become a wild vine?" (Jer 2:21)

Vineyards also call to heart the lover's sigh from the Song of Songs, which in Christian tradition is the allegorical yearning of the soul for God. We read there that "my vineyard,

my very own, is for myself. . . . Make haste, my beloved!"
(Sg 8:12, 14).

Jesus stands within the collective, symbolic, love-soaked
imagery of the vine. "I am the vine," Jesus says, implying
that the vine is neither a political or cultural identity, nor a
religious institution, but Jesus himself and those who abide
in love with him.

Attached to the Christ-vine, we are the people in whom
God dwells. Our hearts make haste to run to the arms of the
beloved.

Conclusion

Contemplation is for everyone, possible everywhere and at
any time, and there are endless ways and places to fall in love
with God.

The desert is first a pliable metaphor for contemplation's
spaces. While barren landscapes still hold transformative
power, deserts are more populated these days. In a technological age, deserts serve as contested sites for cities, nuclear
tests, oil drilling, and pipeline development. As Thomas Merton once wrote, "When man and his money and machines
move out in the desert and dwell there, not fighting the devil
as Christ did, but believing in his promises of power and
wealth . . . then the desert moves everywhere."[19] Deserts are
symbolic for the inner work of purgation and reality confron-
tation that would-be contemplatives must undergo *wherever*
we find ourselves.

The moment and opportunity of contemplation, Jeremiah
reveals, is embedded in political context, crisis, and Empire.
Those who sense God's searing call in their bones are often
not the comfortable, status-quo upholders, but margin

dwellers who remain at the "edge of the inside." They are the ones who mourn, weep, and place their bodies in witness to the systemic injustices of climate change, racism, violence, and poverty.

Contemplation is not a self-improvement scheme but a journey of true aliveness. The loving flow of abiding in the vine of Christ is what brings such fruitful vitality to us. Jesus, along with mystic voices from other religious traditions, tells us that our spiritual aliveness rests on awakening to intrinsic connectedness. The pressure-cooker of my professional and parenting lives nudges me towards such aliveness, all while the busy grind of working moms and dads serves not as a barrier, but a bridge towards true identity in God.

Through desert sojourns, mountaintop revelations, laments of loss, and entwined vines, God the generative Source, the ever-brooding Spirit, and the universal Christ bear transforming fruit.

Notes

1. Novalis, *Philosophical Writings*, trans. and ed. Margaret Mahony Stoljar (Albany: SUNY Press, 1997), 134.

2. Rob Bell, *What Is the Bible? How an Ancient Library of Poems, Letters, and Stories Can Transform the Way You Think and Feel about Everything* (New York: HarperCollins, 2017), 80.

3. Diarmaid MacCulloch, *Silence: A Christian History* (New York: Viking, 2013), 16–17.

4. I use the term *Empire* inspired by Michael Hardt and Antonio Negri's definition: "The concept of Empire posits a regime that effectively encompasses the spatial totality, or reality that rules over the civilized world. No territorial boundaries limit its reign." Michael Hardt and Antonio Negri, "Empire," *The Guardian*, July 15, 2001,

https://www.theguardian.com/world/2001/jul/15/globalisation.businessandmedia.

5. Barbara A. Holmes, *Joy Unspeakable: Contemplative Practices of the Black Church* (Minneapolis: Fortress Press, 2004), 138.

6. See Belden Lane, *The Solace of Fierce Landscapes: Exploring Desert and Mountain Spirituality* (New York: Oxford University Press), 2007.

7. *Strong's Exhaustive Concordance of the Bible, Hebrew and Chaldee Dictionary*, s.v. *midbar* (New York: Methodist Book Concern, 1890), 61.

8. Ulrich W. Mauser, *Christ in the Wilderness* (Naperville, IL: Alec R. Allenson, 1963), 99.

9. Mauser, *Christ in the Wilderness*, 103.

10. David Aberbach, *Imperialism and Biblical Prophecy 750–500 BCE* (London: Routledge, 1993), 12.

11. Richard Rohr, *Eager to Love: The Alternative Way of Francis of Assisi* (Cincinnati: Franciscan Media, 2014), 43.

12. Walter Brueggemann, *The Theology of the Book of Jeremiah* (New York: Cambridge University Press, 2007), 28–29.

13. Campbell Robertson, "A Lynching Memorial Is Opening. The Country Has Never Seen Anything Like It," *New York Times*, April 25, 2018.

14. Evelyn Underhill, *Mysticism: A Study in the Nature and Development of Man's Spiritual Consciousness* (New York: Dutton, 1961), 170.

15. Robert Augustus Masters, *Spiritual Bypassing: When Spirituality Disconnects Us from What Really Matters* (Berkeley: North Atlantic Books, 2010), 1.

16. Abraham Joshua Heschel, *The Prophets* (New York: Harper & Row, 1962), 108–12.

17. Allen Dwight Callahan, *A Love Supreme: A History of the Johannine Tradition* (Minneapolis: Fortress Press, 2005), 60.

18. Novalis, *Philosophical Writings*, 134.

19. Thomas Merton, *Thoughts in Solitude* (New York: Farrar, Straus, and Giroux, 1956), 7.

Contemplation and Social Justice

PHILEENA HEUERTZ

As we gathered at St. Benedict's Monastery in Snowmass, Colorado, in August 2017, I sensed an invitation into deeper reflection on ways in which our contemplative practice nurtures and empowers a compassionate engagement with the struggles in our society and around the world.

Just a couple of days before the historic *life-giving* gathering of younger contemplative leaders, a *deadly* assembly took place in Charlottesville, Virginia. Rage, hate, violence, and tragic death marked a white supremacists' rally. In the end, at least thirty-four people were wounded. One woman was murdered when a demonstrator plowed his car into a group of counterprotestors. Two state troopers also died. The events shook the world. Jessie Smith, one of the participants at Snowmass, is from Charlottesville. I'll never forget how she broke down in grief over the violence and destruction that had taken place in her hometown.

Sadly, when we examine the world around us, we see many areas of turmoil: systemic racial, ethnic, and religious discrimination; human trafficking; sexual exploitation; overconsumption; environmental abuse; and the proliferation and sale of nuclear weapons—just to name a few. Instead of building a world of peace and justice, we seem to be destroying one another and the planet we inhabit.

Our vision for a better world so often becomes clouded with experiences of pain and suffering, oppression and violence, and it is easy to become discouraged. In the face of doubt, despair, and hate, how can we attempt to cultivate and advance a spirit of faith, hope, and love? How can these virtues within us be realized in the world around us? I dare say it's not possible without contemplative practice.

The integration of contemplation and action is absolutely crucial to building a better world, for contemplation nurtures presence. Presence unearths compassion—the soil from which faith, hope, and love can flourish. From that foundation, we can then build the kind of world we all want to live in.

Through meditation or contemplative prayer, we open to these virtues, which allows them to more easily pass through us into the world around us. We can then exercise faith, hope, and love at the level of personal relationship and interaction with others, and at the systemic level when addressing some of the more complex destructive energies at work on a larger scale.

In 1982, the Jesuit theologian Karl Rahner stated emphatically, "The Christian of the future will be a mystic or [s]he will not exist at all."[1] We are that future. If the Christian faith is to have any relevance at all in our time, it must return to its contemplative soul.

Contemplative prayer is so powerful because it unmasks the unconscious mind—the part of us that has the tendency to cause so much harm (intentionally and unintentionally). It's the undigested, unintegrated parts of our unconscious that cause the illusion of separation. The misconception of separation from God and one another makes possible the kind of violence that was at work in Charlottesville that dreadful summer day.

Those unmetabolized parts of ourselves are the fragments that are wounded and afraid, the pieces we repress and hide. Contemplative prayer meets us right where we are—with our fears, wounds, and illusions. Contemplative practice is a meeting with grace. The light of grace exposes what is hidden, hurt, and afraid. Through contemplation, our unconscious anxieties meet the love that casts out all fear. Then our emotional wounds have a chance to heal, reducing the likelihood that we'll project them on others. The illusion that we are separated from God and one another loses its grip. In time, we realize at deepening levels that we are one with God and one another. Realizing our true nature—oneness—then makes all the difference for how we relate to others.

If we want to liberate our world from the cycle of violence and destruction that too often takes over, we must take up regular contemplative practice. Contemplation helps us build a better world by waking us up. Once awakened, regular contemplative practice then helps us stay awake by cultivating in us embodied presence, embodied compassion, and embodied practice.

Waking Up

For the first twenty years of my life after I graduated from college, I codirected an international nonprofit that served impoverished communities around the globe. At its peak, our organization comprised three hundred people serving in thirteen cities of the majority world: urban centers in South and Southeast Asia, Eastern Europe, West Africa, and South America. We worked among survivors of labor and sex trafficking, abandoned children with HIV and AIDS, children living on the streets, destitute widows, child soldiers, and war brides.

But in all my experience with poverty and injustice, I had seen nothing that compared to the kind of human brutality and suffering that I witnessed in West Africa's Freetown, Sierra Leone.

At the time, 60 percent of the country was still controlled by rebel forces, but the ten-year war over blood diamonds was slowly coming to an end. Soldiers were being disarmed and brought into United Nations peacekeeping camps. Refugees from all over the country were pouring into the capital city—survivors of brutal amputation and children displaced from their parents. Both the government and rebel forces used amputation as a tactic for fear and control of the population.

There seemed to be no mercy for this horrific demonstration of war. Young and old people alike were subjected to having one or both arms chopped off. In some cases, sons were forced to commit the grotesque act on their parents. The only consideration given was the audacious choice between "short" or "long" sleeve—indicating where the sever would take place on the arm. These brave and broken people struggled with basic daily chores such as washing, dressing, and embracing loved ones. Many of the men were farmers. They needed both hands to work the land. Their amputations forced them to face the despair of not knowing how they would ever provide for their families again.

As if meeting the adult survivors of this brutality wasn't enough, I met children who also suffered under the wicked knife of their oppressors—one child was only three months old when the soldiers brutalized her. We met her when she was two, struggling to open the shell of a peanut using her one hand pressed against the nub of what was left of her other little arm.

While at the camp for the war-wounded, we met a number of teenage girls who wanted to share their stories with us.

They were desperate for someone, anyone, to do something to respond to their unbearable circumstances. So I bolstered up the courage to listen and bear witness to their pain.

I heard detailed accounts of how the soldiers came to their villages, rounded up their families, sexually assaulted and systematically amputated the limbs of their mothers, and murdered their fathers. I heard how the soldiers then assaulted the young girls, often gang-raped them repeatedly, and forced them to be their "war brides," meaning they'd be subjected to domestic and sexual slavery.

As the girls recounted the sordid details through glassed-over eyes, some of them held their babies—children conceived from the sexual violence they'd endured. I left the camp in a daze. I couldn't believe the horror my new friends had survived. Before that day, I thought I'd seen it all. Prior to this visit to Freetown, I had spent many years helping to establish communities of justice and hope.

In Sierra Leone I looked for someone to blame: the diamond industry, the government, the soldiers, the warlords whose greed led to such human atrocity. Certainly there were systemic structures of injustice at play that were to blame, much like the systems of global economic disparity I had grown familiar with. But as I recalled the stories of the soldiers who brutalized these young girls, I found individual human faces who were responsible and should pay for their crimes. Anger and judgment stirred in me toward the soldiers who had committed such unspeakable acts.

Then I visited the camp for young soldiers who had recently been disarmed. Boys of all ages—as young as five and seven—gathered together to meet with us. That's right, *child* soldiers. And like the young girls, they too wanted to tell their stories.

In moments, a few teenagers were directed to us. How could I bare to sit down with the soldiers who were responsible for the horrifying suffering of the girls I'd met just the day before?

Somehow, I did.

And the boys began to recount similar stories of soldiers invading their villages, the murders of their parents, and being conscripted into war. They remembered being drugged and forced to cut off arms and legs, and to take up weapons that were too heavy for them to carry. And as the war dragged on, they remembered being given girls to violate.

It was all too much for me to bear. Combatants. Just children. Forced to grow up under the warped parental authority of warlords. As I listened to my little brothers, to the suffering they'd endured and the guilt they lived with, and as I remembered the agony of my younger sisters, I was struggling once again to find someone to blame. The soldiers I had so easily judged and convicted the day before were now sitting in front of me with a sea of pain in *their* eyes. It was now not so easy to demonize them.

It's a natural human tendency to look for a scapegoat—someone to blame for suffering and injustice. In the Hebrew scriptures, we learn about the scapegoat as the innocent animal used in religious ritual during Yom Kippur. All the sins of the people were symbolically placed on a lamb, which was then released into the wilderness as a way of cleansing the people of their imperfections and wrongdoings (Lv 16:8–10). This, in a sense, gave them a clean slate to start anew. A short historical study reveals that Greeks and Romans had similar practices, using a goat, a dog, or even women and men as instruments of atonement and cleansing. This resulted in communities casting out, stoning, and sacrificing those deemed unacceptable. Scapegoating is an example of the myth of redemptive violence, common across many cultures and in many Christians' understanding of the crucifixion of Jesus—believing Jesus was the symbolic "goat" needed to placate God. Fr. Richard Rohr has a helpful teaching on this:

> Humans have always struggled to deal with fear and evil by ways other than forgiveness, most often through sacrificial systems. . . .
>
> If your ego is still in charge, you will find a "disposable" person or group on which to project your problems. . . .
>
> *Jesus became the scapegoat to reveal the universal lie of scapegoating.* Note that John the Baptist said, "Behold the Lamb of God, who takes away the *sin* [singular] of the world" (Jn 1:29). It seems "the sin of the world" is ignorant hatred, fear, and legitimated violence.
>
> *Jesus became the sinned-against one to reveal the hidden nature of scapegoating* and so that we would see how wrong people in authority can be—even religious important people (see John 16:8–11 and Romans 8:3).[2]

And so there I was in Freetown surrounded by mass agony, attempting to apply redemptive violence by looking for someone to blame, stone, cast into the wilderness, or crucify. As my heart tore open, I wondered, "Who is responsible for all this suffering? And not only *this* suffering, but who is responsible for *all* the pain in the world?" I wanted someone to blame.

But I couldn't find the culprit. As I traced the lineage of oppressor and victim, it seemed everyone had been victimized.

I had run out of people to project my judgment, so I sub-consciously directed my anger toward God. I wondered, "If people are basically victims victimizing one another, and God created us, then surely God must answer for this. God must be to blame." I thought, "Perhaps God is not all that good after all."

Have you ever felt that way? In the face of despair, have you doubted God's goodness? What blows has life delivered you? An illness perhaps? Or an unwanted divorce? Suffering is suffering, so don't compare yours to someone else's. Instead, consider events that have taken place either in your life or in the life of someone you love. Has it been a struggle to accept those circumstances?

Those many years ago, facing the trauma of a nation torn apart by war, I found myself plunged into a crisis of faith. What I had learned about God growing up in the Protestant pews of Indiana was radically challenged in the face of human need in Sierra Leone. My worship had dried up. I had no words to pray. Scripture no longer inspired me. And God seemed painfully silent.

I was afraid. I didn't know how to engage such silence. I thought something must be wrong with me. I felt as if I didn't have enough faith; or even worse, something must be terribly wrong with God.

Thankfully, Fr. Thomas Keating came into my life right on time.

Early one spring Saturday morning, my husband's spiritual director left a voicemail inviting the two of us to have dinner with his beloved teacher, an elderly monk that we'd never heard of named Thomas Keating. We were mesmerized at dinner by this tall, humble, Gandalf-like figure dressed in a black robe. Turns out, his religious order, the Cistercians, observe a strict rule of silence. It was out of his deep well of silence that his life radiated so much peace and wisdom. Following dinner, Fr. Thomas gave a teaching and closed with a guided Centering Prayer practice.

Fr. Thomas's teaching was like a wellspring to my arid soul. With gentle authority—the kind of credibility that comes from experience—he opened a portal to God's nourishing presence. He helped me realize that I didn't need to be troubled or discouraged by God's *felt* absence and grueling silence. Like an old transistor radio, I just needed to learn how to tune in to a different frequency. After that day, I found courage to give myself to the silence with all of its darkness, questions, doubts, and pain. And it was there, in the great, deafening silence, that I woke up to a deeper realization of God's presence.

The allures, distractions, and pace of our time, coupled with our inner illusions of self, others, and God, threaten to keep us asleep and at bay from the Source of our existence, purpose, and rest. Most of us go through life sleepwalking. It's not easy to wake up. Usually it takes a crisis of some sort to do so: an unexpected career transition, a feared medical diagnosis, a miscarriage, a natural catastrophe. But contemplative prayer also aids the waking process, in a way that is grounded in loving awareness rather than struggle.

In the face of agony in Sierra Leone, my faith fell short. Forgiveness for such horrific wrongs seemed like an impossibility. Healing for my friends and their nation seemed completely out of reach.

When I had a hit a wall and come to the end of myself, contemplative prayer, in the form Centering Prayer, became the only way in which I could attempt to encounter God. There, in solitude, silence, and stillness, I could just show up—as I am with all my doubts, questions, and pain. And over time, the gentle, secret, grace-filled presence of God began to penetrate my being with a love so enormous that it has the power to transform all the pain of the world—beginning with my own.

Embodied Presence: Being with What Is

After years of social justice work, upon returning from my first visit to Sierra Leone, my religious paradigms were severely challenged, and I didn't know where to turn. I didn't know how to relate to God in the midst of massive injustice and tormenting doubts and questions.

Now, I had been a Christian all my life. My father was a pastor, and growing up I attended church three times a week. I learned at an early age to nurture my relationship with Christ through the study of scripture and prayer. Prayer was not new to me. But the way I had been praying wasn't making much of a difference in my life and the lives of my friends suffering at the hands of injustice.

Fr. Thomas taught me how to pray beyond words or thoughts. He taught me the way of pure prayer—being with Jesus in authentic naked self-surrender—just as I am with all of my personal brokenness and with the brokenness of our world that I carry in my heart. He taught me how to pray in such a way that I can make room for the life of Christ to be lived through me, *responding* to the needs of the world instead of *reacting* to the needs and getting overwhelmed and misdirected.

Fr. Thomas aptly says that if we stay a follower of Jesus long enough, the spiritual practices that used to sustain us in our faith will fall short. They won't support us as they used to. It's inevitable. We reach a point in our journey with Christ when we need more. That's what I was experiencing.

Many Christians today have reached that point. Many are longing for more. Our hearts are yearning for a deeper experience of awareness and transformation, shaped and nurtured by God's fierce love for us and all creation.

The Spirituality of the Brain

Life throws us all kinds of curve balls. We never know what's going to happen. Stress in all shapes and sizes comes at us. In life, there will be challenges. That's certain, so we might as well stop resisting. It's how we respond to life's challenges that makes all the difference. Usually we react to life rather than respond to it. Reacting is constrictive. It shuts us down and closes us off. It's isolating. Responding is expansive. It turns us on and opens us up. It helps us connect with others and experience a sense of belonging. Reacting originates from our lowest self, which is controlled by our lower brain.

The lower brain is made up of the reptilian and mammalian brain, or what the contributing author at *Forbes* magazine Christine Comaford calls the "Critter Brain."[3] This part of our brain is concerned with survival. It has limited access to resources. When we are in physical danger, this part of the brain triggers us to fight, flight, or freeze—a very helpful mechanism when our life depends on it. The problem is that too often, this part of our brain dominates in all stressful situations, even when we are not in physical peril. Coping well with various challenges in our life requires the activation of our higher brain.

The neocortex is the higher brain, the most evolved part of the human brain. Comaford refers to this as the "Smart Brain." Specifically, the prefrontal cortex is known as the executive brain. It is able to respond to life rather than react to it. It has full access to resources. The higher brain has capacity for creativity, innovation, solving complex problems, and thinking abstractly. The prefrontal cortex has enabled us to have advanced behaviors such as tool making, language skills, and higher states of consciousness.

The higher brain is well equipped to help us not only manage stress but also live into our highest, truest selves. Contemplative practice helps us develop the habit of being with what is, which then activates our higher brain. In essence, contemplation establishes a new mind in us (Eph 4:23), one that helps us transform from low-level, reactionary people to people who can respond to life with self-control, peace, and compassion.

Embodied Compassion: Being One with All

It is this deeper experience of awareness and transformation—grounded in God's love—that helps us embody compassion in pursuit of social justice. Social injustice is rooted in our refusal to identify with the so-called other. For once we identify with the child soldier, the person who is a different color than us, or the immigrant, we realize that *their* concerns are really *our* concerns. But it's not so easy to dismantle the boundaries we've constructed between one another. This is probably the area in which we most need God's grace. In our global, pluralistic, diverse society, wracked with social unrest, thoughtful Christians long to realize and live out the essence of our Gospel; a Gospel that promises justice, equality, peace, and ultimately belonging.

As we face paramount threats to life together on planet Earth, it doesn't help to fight with one another about our differing opinions, convictions, and interpretations of scripture. Our ideas, beliefs, and words are limited in their ability to find a way forward as loving peacemakers. I like the way Fr. Richard summarizes the limitations of words:

After the Enlightenment in the 17th century, we regressed in many ways as religion wanted to compete with the rational, intelligent thinkers of Europe. The later Protestant Reformation moved forward with this mind as individuals and groups claimed there was only one correct interpretation of every scripture. Catholics looked to the Pope for that one correct interpretation. It's no surprise there are 30,000 Protestant denominations today, and Catholicism became so monarchical. We will never agree on the meanings of words. That's why the Word became flesh, to reveal that words can't get you there. Only experience, love, and relationship can.[4]

Our digital age only makes matters worse. We are inundated with words, opinions, ideas, and information, and it's overwhelming us. We're developing digital addictions that threaten the very fabric our society. Living so many hours of the day attached to our digital devices, we are cut off from personal contact and engagement with one another. We often don't know how to talk to one another, let alone love one another well. Words void of love and wisdom are fruitless.

Addressing social justice begins with our ability to listen to one another—and often with people who are very different from us. We need to make time and space for fewer words, less noise, and more communion with the Divine. This kind of spiritual practice equips us to be in relationship with one another, genuinely listening to one another so we can address some of the most challenging problems of our time.

Contemplative prayer answers this need. Contemplative prayer practices marked by solitude, silence, and stillness are absolutely imperative for Christians who care about our shared planet. Learning to pray with our whole selves beyond words and thoughts, and learning to do this together, makes room for the Holy Spirit to heal the divisions between us, nurture unitive consciousness, and ultimately heal the social ills of our time. Contemplative prayer helps build a society we all want to live in, realizing, as Jesus put it, the reign of God on earth as it is in heaven.

Our digitally addicted lifestyles are draining the life energy from us. We are tired and desperate for practices of solitude, silence, and stillness—prayer practices that still the noise and offer moments of peace and communion with our Creator, the Ground of All Being. Our broken society really can't wait any longer for us to learn to pray beyond words and thoughts— the way of contemplative prayer. Contemplative prayer helps us access that fertile soil of compassion, where faith, hope, and love abound. Through regular contemplation we learn the way of embodying the foundation of essence: compassion. Embodied compassion then helps us live into our inter-connectedness with all.

Embodied Practice: Cultivating a New World from the Inside Out

In solitude, we learn to be present. We learn to be present to ourselves, to God, and to one another. Practicing silence helps us develop the capacity to listen. We learn to listen to ourselves, to God, and to one another. And over time, as we practice stillness, we develop restraint or self-control and are able to discern God's will with greater clarity. This allows us to respond rather than reacting to life.

Curiously, adopting a contemplative or meditation prac-tice directly impacts our overattachment to what Fr. Thomas calls our emotional programs for happiness—that part of our lower brain-self that craves the basic biological needs of power and control, affection and esteem, security and survival.

We need a certain degree of power and control, affection and esteem, security and survival to thrive in life, but life won't meet all of these needs all the time. It is in times when these needs are left wanting that we have to find a healthy way to cope. We need to activate the higher brain, or as Paul would say, find a way to put on "the mind of Christ" (1 Cor 2:16).

These cravings inside us are laid bare in contemplative prayer. Here we identify with Jesus's temptations in the desert. That incredible drama in the gospel illustrates for us the human struggle to know who we are, and the struggle to respond to challenges and temptations from our truest, best selves. In the desert Jesus was tempted toward the same programs for happiness that we are.

When we practice stillness, we practice letting go of power and being in control. When we practice solitude, we practice letting go of being defined and limited by the affection and esteem of others. And when we practice silence, we practice letting go of finding security in what we have.[5] It's clear that we are in need of transformation. We need a new mind and a new way of being in the world. Contemplative practice positions us to receive the inner work of transformation. It is a way for us to cooperate with grace, or as Paul put it, to be conformed to the image of God's son (Rom 8:29). Contemplative prayer then helps us embody the practice of faith, hope, and love in our interactions with the world.

When the disciples asked Jesus how to pray, Jesus instructed them to ask that God's kingdom would come and God's will would be done on earth as it is in heaven. Could we dare to ask God for that? In a world of social injustice, which often includes horrific violence, the only hope is love—the love of God that Jesus embodied. Only love can forgive seventy times seven. Only love can establish unity with people who are different from us. Only love can transform us and our world. May we be compelled to give ourselves to love through contemplative prayer practice, allowing ourselves to open to the Divine so that we might heal our world.

Simply put, contemplative prayer builds a just society because it cultivates love of God, self, and neighbor. Ultimately contemplation creates the conditions for us to be transformed. And as we are transformed, the world is transformed.

It's been many years since I made that first visit to war-torn Freetown. My life has taken a few turns. I no longer codirect the international nonprofit that took me to West Africa. I now have very little contact with the people I once knew there.

One of the greatest challenges in my life at that time was coming to terms with my limitations. There is only so much I can do. There is a massive sea of need in the world, and it has been crucial to discern how I can best channel my energies to respond to those needs. What that meant for me was doing everything I could to establish a local community that could respond on a daily basis to the survivors of war in Freetown. That was within my means. It was also within my means to teach the leaders of that community contemplative practice. Today, the children and young people who attend my former organizations' programs practice meditation in addition to receiving education, and eventually learning a trade to make a living. They are healing from the inside out.

As for my ongoing response to social injustice at home and abroad, it became clear to me that I could best serve by helping social justice activists integrate contemplation with their action. So most of my time is now spent teaching people contemplative practice and offering spiritual direction to help them discern their own most authentic response to the needs of the world.

You see, contemplation doesn't take us out of the world; it refines our engagement with the world. Like a laser beam of light, contemplation helps us concentrate our energies into the most effective and beneficial contribution we can offer. Without contemplation, our energies are diffused, and our impact and effectiveness weakened.

It's up to us to build a better world. You and I each have a part to play. Contemplation helps us discover that purpose and stay faithful to the contribution we are made to offer.

Notes

1. Karl Rahner, *Concern for the Church*, vol. 20 of *Theological Investigations* (New York: Crossroad, 1981), 149.

2. Richard Rohr, "The Scapegoat Mechanism," Center for Action and Contemplation, April 30, 2017, https://cac.org/the-scapegoat-mechanism-2017-04-30; Rohr, Richard, "The Myth of Redemptive Violence," Center for Action and Contemplation, May 1, 2017, https://cac.org/myth-redemptive-violence-2017-05-01; emphasis in original.

3. Christine Comaford, "Hijack! How Your Brain Blocks Performance," Forbes, October 21, 2012, https://www.forbes.com/sites/christinecomaford/2012/10/21/hijack-how-your-brain-blocks-performance/#625d7bb02b7b.

4. Richard Rohr, "Wisdom's Way of Knowing," Center for Action and Contemplation, January 15, 2015, https://cac.org/beyond-words-2015-01-15.

5. For a more robust exploration of the impact of solitude, silence, and stillness, see Christopher L. Heuertz, *The Sacred Enneagram: Finding Your Unique Path to Spiritual Growth* (Grand Rapids, MI: Zondervan, 2017).

Contemplation and the Connections of Life

LEONARDO CORRÊA

About ten years ago, I was at a point in my life when my job as a journalist had become stagnant and heavy. I was living in Porto Alegre, in southern Brazil, where I was born and raised. I was on the verge of burnout and deeply skeptical about my life; my tendency toward perfectionism had led to difficulty sleeping and lots of stress. Emotionally, the end of a relationship had hardened my heart a little more. Then I encountered Christian meditation—or it found me.

Spiritually, up to this point, my journey had followed more or less along these lines: God was a supreme one to appeal to when fear was pressing around me. I remember, when I was a kid, many nights I fell asleep repeating a phrase of supplication. It was something like "Please, don't let me or my family ever die." (This practice of repetition during prayer would come back later, in a transformed way, when I found meditation.) But also God was a ubiquitous judge, before whom I placed heavy burdens of guilt every time my conscience pointed out mistakes or sins. In short, my religious experience was not very healthy; it was a product of both a psychological fear of death and social conditioning.

As an adult, fear and guilt as driving forces of my religious practice weakened a bit. Fear and guilt were still there, but I dealt with them as most people usually do: hanging out with friends, drinking, keeping myself distracted and busy.

I eventually reached a point where passing time with the routines of work and leisure, spending time with online relationships, and carrying an excessive workload raised questions for me. Was life just about having a responsible adult life, working, earning enough to survive, if possible, finding someone to love, then growing old and dying after a few years? Was life really just about all that?

Late one evening, I was returning home from work. With my headphones on, I was flipping radio stations and suddenly paused at the Radio Aliança, a local Catholic radio station. Marcelo, a doctor, was talking about meditation and the idea of starting a new group. I memorized his name and email. When I got home, I sent a note inquiring about meditation.

Since the beginning, meditation made sense for me. I felt something I would hear many times from other meditators: it was like coming home, just a natural thing. The silence was always a need for me, something that holds within itself a special gift, deep and mysterious. I remember the simple fact of doing ordinary things in silence—washing dishes or lying down looking at the ceiling, for example—had a healing effect on me.

Out of simple grace I was quickly able to build a daily practice of meditation twice a day. I started practicing in a weekly group, and I went on retreats with the World Community for Christian Meditation (WCCM) director Fr. Laurence Freeman, OSB. In a natural evolution of things, I ended up leaving my job in 2011 and going to live in Meditatio House in London for a year. It was my oblate year, a formation stage in a process that some meditators in our community undertake to live in the spirit of the Rule of St. Benedict.

When I left a steady job to go live in a Christian meditation community in London, everything seemed separate, fragmented: my old life was behind me—my home, family, town; even the language I was talking was no longer the same.

When I returned to Brazil following my year in London, I started to work as the WCCM director of communications. On my return I felt that I brought back with me a better sense of being connected to a whole and a connection with the world and the human family. It brought me to a new way of working, a new way of living day to day. I can feel that connection, whether I meditate every morning with my wife, Marci, or when I meditate with my group on Mondays in Porto Alegre or with groups online, with people who can be in Europe, the Middle East, the United States, or anywhere.

Meditation helped me, step by step, transform my way of seeing and living. It works because it puts one in contact with the goodness and love at the center of our nature. The expansion of this goodness, of the love that we have in the center of ourselves, is transforming. Even if one does not give God's name to that nature, the practice itself nurtures one's life, because we experience the transformation of getting in touch with the expansive love and goodness at our center. As the Benedictine monk and interspiritual pioneer Bede Griffiths describes:

> All the meditation groups throughout the world are composed of people who are searching for this deeper meaning, this reality of God in their own lives. Father John refers to this movement to recover our capacity for God as the "new creation." This capacity, innate in every human being, has been obscured through sin, that is through alienation from one's own true

being. Sin is alienation. It is failing to know oneself
as one really is through alienation from one's true
being, from reality, from God. The new creation is
the renewal of our being which takes place when we
awake to who we are.[1]

Meditation helps to "clear the doors of perception." It
helps us recognize that our isolation from the Creator exists
only in our misinterpretation, our misunderstanding. We
can call it sin. Meditation is this work of cleansing, purify-
ing the eyes of the heart (as St. Augustine said), which alone
can "see" the kingdom. "You cannot observe the kingdom,"
Jesus says in the Gospel, because the kingdom is within and
among us (Lk 17:20). Contemplative practice shows us in an
empirical way how we can "see" the kingdom in ourselves,
which is invisible to the eyes normally.

Seeing the Connections

For me, there is always hope that the world can be better,
not in the sense that one day there will be no more suffering,
inequality, or violence, but in recognizing ourselves as part of
a whole, as part of the same human family.

I not only feel more connected to those I meditate with in
the present moment, but I also feel connected with an ancient
Christian tradition, with John Cassian, St. Benedict, and so
many other Christian contemplatives throughout history.
Having the opportunity to take part in the New Contemplative Leaders Exchange in 2017, in Snowmass, Colorado,
allowed me to meet other Christian contemplatives, with similarities and diversity, and the same aim to make the world a
more peaceful place.

I can say I feel the connection also with meditators from other traditions even older than the Christian one. Fr. Laurence mentions a meeting he had with an Australian Aboriginal during one of his lectures on Christian meditation around the world:

> There was a Christian Aborigine who was in the audience. He came to me afterward and thanked me. He said, "Do you know? My people have been meditating for forty thousand years. We call it *didgeri*, which is a silent nonquestioning awareness, the harmony with the world around us. They go to a rock or near the river." He said, "I just need to sit beside the river and feel the flow of the river, and we open ourselves to that presence in nature."[2]

Being open to the "presence in nature" is exactly what we do during daily meditation. We do not elaborate complex thoughts, beautiful words, or supplications and dramatic requests: we *are* only before "the presence," that is, always here and now.

I believe all these different ways to express and feel part of a whole is the natural effect of meditation. As John Main said, the "opening of our heart is as natural as the opening of a flower." What unites us is the simplicity of practice and the joy of recognizing ourselves in each other during this pilgrimage.

> Meditation and the constant return to it, every day of your life, is like cutting a pathway through to reality. Once we know our place, we begin to see very much in a new light because we have become who we really are. And becoming who we are, we can now see everything

as it is and so begin to see everyone else as they are. The truest wonder of meditation is that we may even begin to see God as God is. Meditation is therefore a way to stability. We learn the practice and from the experience how to be rooted in our essential being. We learn to be rooted in our essential being to be rooted in God, the author and principle of all reality.[3]

But the world is so full of worries and distractions so that most of the time, we are not able to perceive it. "God is at home, it is we who have gone out for a walk," said the medieval German theologian, philosopher and mystic Meister Eckhart. Meditation is simply coming back home from that walk, given most of the time by our own minds. Ultimately it is to return every second to the mantra, the word-prayer, to the "only thing necessary," as Jesus says to Martha in Luke 10:42.

Additionally, if we consider the journey of meditation as a reconnection with reality, with nature and with our own nature, we must also see it as a journey of healing and reintegration.

In this relatively short period of about a decade in which I have begun to meditate, I have realized my personal process of healing and reintegration: physical, psychological, and spiritual aspects that become healthier. There is more awareness of the grace of my body, of the way I eat and move, even an awareness of my perception, my senses—how I see beauty or listen to music, for instance.

Psychologically, I experience less anxiety and fear when the ego acts in a way that is not healthy. Spiritually, I experience less religious guilt, and I trust that I am always loved, even when I am not exactly a "good boy." I have also seen beautiful examples of fellow pilgrim meditators in the WCCM community who have come to a deeper sense of wholeness through meditation. For example, we have groups that meditate as a way to practice the 11th step program in a 12-step program of recovery. This is their mission statement:

> Step 11—"Sought through prayer and meditation to improve our conscious contact with God as we understood Him, praying only for knowledge of his will for us and the power to carry that out."
>
> Addiction & Recovery outreach shares an ancient path of contemplative prayer as a way to practice the 11th step. We are not a replacement for nor are we affiliated with any 12-step program. All are welcome, faith or none, 12-step or not.[4]

Since Meditatio, the outreach to take the fruits of meditation to secular society, was launched, WCCM has promoted a series of seminars on education, leadership, health, mental health, addiction, and other subjects.

In Ireland, Laurence Freeman and Dr. Barry White, a physician and meditator from Dublin, have worked together to bring meditation to health-care professionals. Courses were promoted on the practice of meditation in the Royal College of Physicians of Ireland, and more recently a trial was conducted at a Dublin hospital to identify effects of meditation on professionals in the emergency room, which has a very high burnout rate. It is not surprising that the first results pointed to a reduction in the burnout rate.

A few years ago, I visited a meditation group for homeless people in Boston. It is a project led by the Episcopal Priest and meditator Rev. Cristina Rathbone. It was moving to see the simplicity and benefits that the practice gave to people who have a very tough daily routine. One of the people I interviewed, Paul, told me that meditation was one of the few moments he could close his eyes without fear that he would be beaten or robbed. Talking with Cristina, I was struck by how she used the word *equalizer* to classify meditation. Of course, the simple practice of meditation does not solve the social and economic problem evidenced by homeless people. But I have no doubt that it gives these men and women a resilience and strength to try to improve their life situation. It also gives them dignity and a sense of community, which is no small thing. We see works similar to Cristina's in several other parts of the world.

Another group of people on the margins of society who have benefited from meditation is the incarcerated. These are transformative stories, such as that of our Meditation in Prison coordinator, James Bishop. He spent years in a California prison and found meditation through the work of a chaplain. Years later, when he gained his freedom, he wrote *A Way in the Wilderness: A Commentary on the Rule of Benedict for the Physically and Spiritually Imprisoned.*[5] As a WCCM oblate and lecturer, he often says that meditation made him aware that he lived in a self-made prison all his life, and he ended up finally finding freedom while he was in prison.

Going back to the idea of equalizer, we can say that meditation also helps the rich and powerful in their walks toward reintegration. As the Gospel says, it is easier for a camel to go through the eye of a needle than for a rich man to enter the kingdom. But it is not impossible if this rich person experiences the poverty of spirit that the practice of meditation feeds. We see this in the corporate world, with people seeing the value of meditation as a way to train better leaders, and not just for more profit (although there are many examples of an attempt to commercialize meditation, which I believe will not succeed). There are sincere people who, from their own experience, understand that meditation can promote more humane, more equitable work environments.

In this line I can highlight the Meditation and Leadership course for MBA students at Georgetown University in Washington DC. This has been taught by Fr. Laurence and Bertrand Bouhour, a French meditator who lives in the United States. Students are encouraged to build a daily practice for six weeks, regardless of religion or belief. The results have been of real benefit and life change for the students.

Another example of meditation helping leaders is the founding father of Singapore, Lee Kuan Yew, who died in 2015. He discovered meditation in the last years of his life, through Peter Ng, WCCM's Singapore coordinator. He also had several meetings with Fr. Laurence, who helped him develop his practice of meditation. As Lee Kuan Yew reflected, "I am not a spiritual person. For me the value of meditation is not so much the spiritual values, but the value it has in helping me to solve problems. But undoubtedly, in the long run, it must alter a person's character."[6]

He was very honest in saying he did not practice as a spiritual activity. But during the interview, he admitted that meditation helped him realize that there is a true self, different than a public self. For me, this is an experience of interiority, a spiritual experience, even if he did not use this language.

Meditating in All Stages of Life

The WCCM community puts much effort into education, particularly through encouraging meditation in schools. Teaching this gift to children is something urgent these days. "The question for teachers is not why should we teach meditation in schools, but why on earth don't we?" Fr. Laurence says.

It is truly touching to see how much this sharing of the gift of meditation with children has grown from pioneering work in schools in an entire diocese in Townsville, Australia, through thousands of schools in the United Kingdom, Ireland, Canada, and the United States, as well as Fiji, the Caribbean region, Mexico, and South America. Across the world, the value of meditation in schools is realized by many communities. Generally, when schools begin to incorporate meditation into their curricula, the first challenge they face is how to train teachers and enable them to experience meditation themselves. Once the training and practice of teachers is achieved, then the teachers are ready to pass the practice to the students.

The growing momentum of promoting meditation in schools speaks to its transformative power. The practice of meditation improves students' attention and relationships, reduces bullying, and harmonizes the school environment in general. Above all, it gives children an unforgettable experience of what is to be found within themselves. Over time as we become adults and our lives become complex, we lose that gift. But children can meditate and enjoy meditation, and they often take this practice home, transforming the family environment as well.

Even at the end of life, meditation is a practice that can be learned. As Fr. Laurence says, "The practice can be done from childhood to deathbed."[7] The practice of meditation helps us see death more naturally, part of the life and stage of transformation. As a child, when I discovered that death existed, I tried to find a solution to it, to discover what it meant. With parents who were psychologists, the path of illusion or simple denial of death was not a path I could take. The practice of meditation helps us all face death in a new way.

I am reminded of a person I met a few years ago. Anne McDonnell, from the United Kingdom, and her husband, Mark, founded and ran Noggs Barn, a contemplative space in their garden for meditation and retreat days. In her last years, she shared her journey facing terminal cancer in some blog posts and with a small book. She writes:

> I have touched on hints of an eternal dimension while meditating. In paying silent attention to the present moment I find a sense of moving beyond the confines of time into a place of infinite expansion. I am here in the "now," yet that "now" moves on and out into an eternal "now," present in this moment yet also stretching away into endlessness. Eternity becomes recognisable, yet is forever elusive. It is beyond any human ability to comprehend, yet intimations of it come in moments when we stop to really see and really look. I find this a freeing experience as it becomes even more evident that to try and contain time or to have rigid definitions of what should be happening, is to close a door; then I am not open to the creative potential that this moment represents.[8]

Anne passed away peacefully on All Saints Day, November 1, 2015.

These are only brief reflections and descriptions of what I have lived, especially in the last ten years, since I began to meditate. My work with WCCM as the director of communications has meant that I am able to help WCCM communities communicate the love that is experienced through the practice of meditation. I found that my vocation resonates with what John Main writes:

The practicality of the message of Christian meditation is that by our fidelity to the pilgrimage and by
our openness to the indwelling we love to understand
that the great work in life is to communicate this
love, to help others to see by its light. If we ourselves
understand this and see and judge everything by the
light of this love, then we have learned to live our
lives with supreme compassion. The way of meditation is at the same time the way of compassion, of
simplicity and joy.[9]

Serving as a communicator for WCCM, I am working to
"help others to see by its light," as John Main says. Probably
I am the one that most benefits from this work. As I said in
the beginning, one of my personal faults—my "internal lug-
gage"—is perfectionism. But even when this tendency from
time to time comes to surface, I am now able to notice that,
and then hopefully I keep going without getting paralyzed
by the ego-fed voices of fear. I can notice perfectionism, too,
in a world more and more interconnected, where image and
reputation are the most valuable things; where especially the
younger ones—living in a time when it's never been so easy
to be in touch, at least in technological terms—seem to feel so
isolated, so miserable.

We need to arrive at an encounter that apps and devices
cannot attain: we need to meet our real selves on human
terms. Then we will be able to meet the other without fear,
competition, or prejudice. That is why one of the key quotes
by John Main is "Meditation creates community." In a mysterious and amazing way, this is what is happening with our
WCCM community, since the first weekly meditation group
started with Fr. John in London.

I feel my world has expanded greatly and continues to expand. Of course, this too—as my own journey and as for us all—is a work in progress. It will always be, and that is what makes it so meaningful. There is a lot to do—we only need to look to the world around us, and to the craziness of the global context. But I believe there is hope, if we create opportunities for people to stop and just be, and to feel the connection (or the reconnection). Then they will know they are never alone: It is not about you against the world. It is about us, as a whole humanity.

Notes

1. Bede Griffiths, *Meditation & The New Creation in Christ*, Spiritual Masters Series (London: Medio Media, 2007), 2–3; www.wccm.org/sites/default/files/users/images/PDF/A07BedeGriffiths.pdf.

2. Laurence Freeman, "What Is Meditation?" World Community for Christian Meditation, accessed April 30, 2018, https://www.wccm.org/content/what-meditation.

3. John Main, *The Heart of Creation* (Norwich, UK: Canterbury Press, 2007), 10.

4. "Meditatio: Meditation as an 11th Step Practice," World Community for Christian Meditation, accessed April 30, 2018, http://wccm.org/content/meditatio-meditation-11th-step-practice.

5. James Bishop, *A Way in the Wilderness: A Commentary on the Rule of Benedict for the Physically and Spiritually Imprisoned* (New York: Continuum, 2012).

6. Lee Kuan Yew, "Why Meditate?" *Reflections by Leaders Who Meditate* (2014; London: Medio Media, 2014), DVD.

7. Freeman, "What Is Meditation?"

8. Anne Mc Donnell, *Meditation & Dying* (London: Medio Media, 2015).

9. Main, *Heart of Creation*, 61.

Embodied Contemplation

MARK KUTOLOWSKI

God yearns to bring each of us fully into divine life: soul, spirit, and body. As individuals within the Christian contemplative movement, we have yet to open to the full depths of transformation in Christ. We have beautifully articulated the expansion of spiritual awareness, purification of heart, and elevation of mind and consciousness that occur in contemplative prayer, yet the body remains largely on the sidelines of otherwise comprehensive expositions on contemplative prayer and life. For example, Fr. Thomas Keating's landmark book is titled *Open Mind, Open Heart: The Contemplative Dimension of the Gospel.*[1] What about "Open Body"? I believe the body can and must be incorporated into the transformative journey in the next generation of contemplative practice.[2]

When we gathered at the New Contemplative Leaders Exchange at St. Benedict's Monastery in Snowmass, we touched upon the need for greater embodiment in prayer, though my sense is that we barely scratched the surface of this vast and critically misunderstood topic. Three times during our gathering we had body prayer sessions, each led by a different member of our group, yet these sessions were optional and merely fifteen minutes long. Our schedule reflected the state of body practice in the contemplative movement. In the movement as a whole, there is a vague awareness that body integration matters, but our attention is much more focused on cultivating intellectual understanding, emotional healing, and social change as fruits of contemplative practice.

When I have asked senior contemplative teachers about the body, I have heard responses ranging from the deflective "I just don't go there," to the overly basic "It's good to stretch or go for a walk to relax before meditation," to abdication to other traditions, "Have you tried yoga?" These responses highlight the current poverty of the Christian contemplative tradition in relation to the body. This poverty is all the more agonizing held next to the central role of bodily healing in the ministry of Jesus, in the Acts of the Apostles, and in the first several hundred years of the church.[3] I believe that today we have an awareness of the body in contemplative practice that is similar to the Christian awareness of meditation in the 1960s and 1970s. In that era, when drawn to interior silence, many believed they had to take up Zen, Transcendental Meditation, or another Eastern discipline to learn meditation. We have since recovered an authentic lineage of interior practice in the Western contemplative tradition. However, in the realm of the body, we have no public expression of a Christian practice of a similar depth. If Christians practice at all, they generally take up yoga, tai chi, or qigong. They lack access to an indigenous Christian body discipline.

I have had a lifelong interest in the relationship of the body to spiritual growth. At age twenty I had a serious spinal injury that left me unable to sit up for more than a few minutes at a time for several months. After exhausting conventional medical options, in desperation I began working with a qi gong master,[4] training my body to direct the flow of qi, or bioenergy, for self-healing. I recovered quickly, and

I became fascinated with the study of subtle energies. I later spent a year living in Malaysia, studying at a medical qigong center that relied heavily on silent meditation combined with body awareness to both heal clients and enhance their spiritual awareness. At that same time, I began a twice daily Centering Prayer practice, which I have continued for the past eighteen years.

As I studied the writings of Fr. Thomas Keating, I discovered close parallels between the interior purification process Fr. Keating described in contemplative prayer and the physical healing process I observed in medical qigong clients. Like many Western Christians trying to bring the body into prayer, I had developed a "dual practice" of an Eastern body discipline (yoga, tai chi, or qigong) coupled with a Christian meditative practice (Centering Prayer). After many years of training I concluded that there are inherent limits to a body discipline that emerges from a different spiritual and philosophical system than one's primary spiritual home. At a subtle level, the energies that flow through body, soul, and spirit in spiritual practice have an "imprint" that is distinct, and the practice of one tradition or lineage shapes these imprints in ways that are unique.

With a desire to integrate my contemplative lineage and my body discipline, I began to explore the possibility of a particularly Christian tradition of body prayer. In 2008, I began training with Vladimir Vasiliev in Systema, a Russian health practice and martial art. This practice emerges from the Russian Orthodox worldview, and many of the Systema breathing practices have developed from the breath and heartbeat prayers of Orthodox hesychast prayer disciplines. Through my integration of Systema training with contemplative prayer, I have continued to explore the principles of body transformation within Christian contemplation. I have come to believe we can develop a contemplative Christian body practice. Such a practice would provide immense benefits both to individual practitioners and to the entire contemplative movement. It offers a way to fill in the "missing link" between interior prayer and outward action, by providing a means for the literal embodiment of the fruits of contemplation in the physiology of the disciple.[5] This embodiment would precede and empower the expression of contemplation in action that is so urgently needed in our era.

A Vision of Divine-Human Unity

As my journey of embodied faith continues, bodily experience itself has become a primary teacher. One aspect of this is that I frequently experience a full body surge of energy (which is also perceived as light when I close my eyes) after receiving Eucharist. One Sunday in late 2015, this occurred in a particularly intense way. After receiving the elements, I came back to the pew to kneel. As I knelt in prayer, I felt a sensation like light coming down from above, pushing through my head and slowly, over several minutes, penetrating down through my body and out through my feet. I was aware that the light-sensation moved more slowly in areas where I had tension in my body and more freely and smoothly where I was relaxed. After a few moments of this sensation, I saw a vision: A human form, with arms raised in prayer, extended both overhead and out to the sides of the body like a Y. Two channels of light flowed down from heaven through the center or core of the body—one slightly to the left, one slightly to the right—and continued into the earth. In the earth, the channels circled outward and back up, into two return channels coming up from the earth and through the person's hands going into the heavens, into the sky. These channels then flowed back around and connected into the downward channels of light—like two giant ocean currents.

I had the intuitive sense that this was an image of the human body's natural role as connector between the realms of spirit and matter. Divine light comes through us into the earth, and then the praises and offerings of the earth come back through us to God. In this vision, the human person was both the vessel for divine light coming to the earth (descent) and the agent through which the forces or elements of matter are raised up into the Infinite (ascent). In the moment of vision, I understood this to be the meaning of Christ as the Divine-human One.[6] Jesus's body was completely human and completely divinized. It is a restoration of our original human nature in the image and likeness of God,[7] and at the same time a foreshadowing of the restoration of humanity in the new creation. To the extent that our bodies are liberated and integrated into the process of transformation in Christ, our bodies can become the living link between the Infinite and the finite, between spirit and matter.[8] In the vision, I understood this as the very reason human beings are incarnate on this plane—not to ascend permanently to the world of spirit beyond matter[9] but to be the conscious link between heaven and earth in a way that supports harmonious flow of matter into spirit and spirit into matter.[10] Jesus's own resurrected body, fully united to the Infinite yet engaged directly with the world of matter,[11] is the template of this role of a fully liberated human body in creation. He is, as the New Testament says, the "first fruits" of the new creation, and we are called to become like Him.[12]

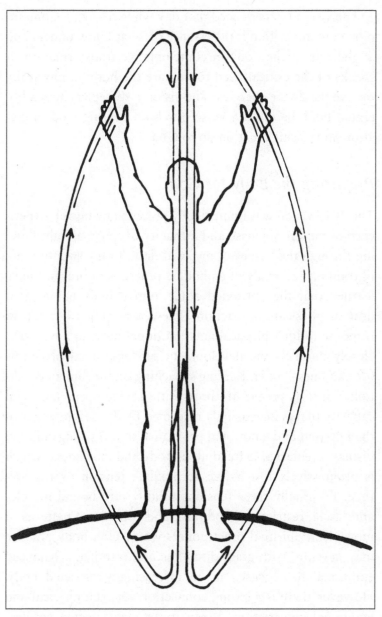

Figure 4. A vision of Divine-human unity (Image by Amanda Sisk.)

The vision I experienced that day while receiving Communion contains within it the essence of what I now understand as the role of the body in contemplative transformation. It speaks of the critical need to prepare the body to physically receive the divine energies. The vision also depicts how a liberated body becomes a vessel for both bearing God in creation and raising creation up to God.

Preparing the Body for God

The 2015 vision was immediately preceded by my felt experience of the varying ease and difficulty of spiritual light flowing through the tissues of my own flesh. In my twenty years of training and study of embodied practices of prayer, I have learned that the untrained adult human body has a great deal of physical compaction. These restrictions develop in response to life's physical and emotional hurts in a way that closely parallels the development of "emotional programs for happiness" in Fr. Keating's teaching on the human condition.[13] Just as people are born with a wide-open emotional capacity that is increasingly restricted by the development of the false self and emotional programs, so too young children display a remarkable freedom of body and movement, which is progressively lost as we accumulate tension over a lifetime. Eventually these tensions solidify into bound muscles and fascia, restricted blood flow, and constricted patterns of movement. Spiritual practitioners who lack a body practice may develop, with great discipline and training, a balanced emotional life encased in an increasingly restricted body. However, there is a strong connection between physical and emotional constriction. When my students regain softness in their body through Systema training, I invariably see a parallel increase in their emotional ease and flexibility. They become more able to respond to emotional stressors without collapsing into the instinctual fight-flight-freeze response. In a similar way, an unbalanced inner life typically leads to stiff and conditioned patterns of movement. Healing in either realm brings the possibility of greater freedom in the other.[14]

I propose that preparing the body to receive the Spirit of God must be included as an essential part of contemplative training within the broader Christian tradition. This body training would involve learning to soften the muscles and to relax the body in a way that parallels the opening of the heart in silent prayer. It would include the integration of breathing, posture, movement, and relaxation[15] to heal physical imbalances. The practice would support deep physical well-being and especially heal and strengthen the nervous system so that the bodies "circuits" are prepared to handle the great intensity of energies that are opened up in serious spiritual practice. When the tissues are open and relaxed, the divine energies flow through our bodies in a way that is unmistakably physical. Physical health and vitality, a kinetic awareness of spiritual realities, and the ability to heal others are natural fruits of this opening.

From reviewing ancient and contemporary Christian spiritual literature and the lives of the saints, and observing the spiritual journeys of many, I see two possible outcomes of neglecting this physical preparation. The first, and more common, is that we encounter the deepest presence of God as "out there" in a realm separate from our bodies. When we enter into deep interior silence, we ignore or disassociate from our bodies and experience the spiritual level of being in a disembodied fashion.[16] We may talk about "integrating contemplation and action," but practically we only will our body into action, motivated by the spirit. The possibility of the spirit *physically* pouring through the body is not even considered! Within this "body-less" experience of contemplative practice, we may experience profound awakening of the spirit and healing of the emotional field,[17] but our bodies are largely unchanged.[18] We have failed to fully integrate our contemplative practice in a way that honors the incarnational foundation of Christian practice. I believe this is the most common experience of people who have taken up a regular contemplative discipline in our time.

There is a second danger of undertaking the spiritual journey without integrating the body and preparing for transformation. This fate seems to be reserved for those with incredible levels of devotion and openness to God and is witnessed largely in the lives of some saints. When the soul is radically open to God, and the body is largely unprepared, the sheer "voltage" of divine life that flows through the body can overload the untrained nervous system. The result, I believe, is seen in the experience of many great saints who had intense experiences of God, often worked miracles (including miraculous healings of others), and yet were coupled with frequent sickness, physical infirmities, and early death. It is as if their bodies could not handle the sheer intensity of divine power moving through them, much like the electric wiring in a house melting down when the energy of a lightning bolt passes through it. Contemporary Systema master Mikhail Ryabko describes this possibility and a potential remedy: "Prayer brings us to God. Getting closer to God is like coming up to a river of love and light of such intensity that if the body and psyche are not properly prepared, it can rip you apart! The body is strengthened, purified, and prepared for prayer by proper breathing practice."[19]

I am curious about the role the absence of systematic body preparation had in lives of the saints Francis of Assisi, Anthony of Padua, Casimir Jagiellon, Aloysius Gonzaga, Therese of Lisieux, and many others.[20] Many Christian theologians have linked the suffering of the body to participation in Christ's own suffering, and have viewed the physical infirmities of the devout as a bearing of Christ's likeness. From my perspective, the experience of bodily participation in (or "bearing of") the suffering of the world is a natural aspect of advanced contemplation. What I view as unnecessary is allowing this experience to destroy a body through manifestation as disease. I believe this frequently happens to a physiologically unprepared body when the person begins to experience a spiritual participation in the sufferings of Christ and of the human family. It is a result of the stagnation of these forces in the body of the contemplative, rather than an inevitable result of sharing in the sufferings of Christ. A body that is prepared is able to bear a far greater energetic load of vicarious suffering and yet not be destroyed by the process. The more prepared our nervous system, the greater our ability to experience pain and dis-ease passing through our bodies without manifesting as disease.[21] We must always remember that while Christ bore our infirmities, his body never succumbed to disease. Rather, his body was a divine instrument for liberating others from disease. Why shouldn't the experience of his disciples be similar?[22]

The ideal time to start such a body practice is childhood, before major constrictions have begun to set in. If children were initially trained in a body-based discipline, the neural pathways could remain relatively clear, and the training in physical softness could be preparation for the subtler spiritual opening that takes place in a contemplative discipline such as Centering Prayer or Christian meditation practice. Then, when the intuitive faculties come online more fully around the classic age of initiation (roughly the midteens), the students would be introduced to a regular discipline of silent prayer. At this time, they would be ready to navigate the spiritual journey with nervous systems and bodies that were well prepared for the work that lay ahead. For the rest of us, it is never too late to do remedial work to bring the body back into our spiritual practice. Doing so will greatly enhance the integration of our spiritual practice with the rest of our lives.

Bearing God into Creation, Raising Creation into God

When the body is healed, opened, and purified, it becomes a vessel of divine Life, much as I saw in the vision described above. After a certain level of integration is accomplished through exercises, relaxation, and conscious breathing (usually a few years), prayer itself becomes an embodied practice, and accumulated physical tensions are released regularly and powerfully in daily prayer.[23] With additional years of silent prayer, a long-term fruit of body-integrated contemplation is that the body begins to take on what I believe is its natural state: the state capable of bearing divine energies into the realm of creation and of lifting up creation into God.

In the movement of descent, the practitioner experiences divine Life descending through the body of its own accord. Nothing is done to invite this, but there is a frequent felt experience of spiritual essence settling or "sinking" through the channel of the body and beyond the body into the earth itself and out into all creation. It is as if the body has become a hollow tube, where light flows down and out into the world without any effort on the part of the practitioner.

In the movement of ascent, there is a spontaneous desire to lift all of creation up to God in prayer. The body of the practitioner becomes something like a magnet for the life, love, and longing of all matter, and with upstretched arms sends this flow up through their body into the Infinite.[24] When body and soul are clear, this desire is as natural as breathing. The lover of God finds herself acting as a sort of "priest of creation," channeling divine love from the Infinite into the finite and offering embodied, particular love from the creatures back to their Source.

Together, the movements of the ascent and descent of love, moving through the transformed human body, become a sort of second spiritual circulatory system. It accompanies a person wherever they walk, and they act as a source of blessing and integration to both the human and nonhuman worlds they traverse. I believe this is what Jesus was referring to when he said, "Blessed are the peacemakers, for they will be called children of God" (Matthew 5:9). The Hebrew word Jesus used in this teaching, *shalom*, commonly translated as "peace," means the drawing together in unity of all that is separate or fractured. The term *child of God* means one who bears or manifests God's own life and identity in this plane of reality. This is exactly what a mature body-integrated contemplative does: their body becomes a channel through which divine *shalom* breathes out into the world of matter and through which the life of the world is also taken back into the realm of God.[25]

Principles of a Christian Contemplative Body Practice

I am confident that one day the Christian community will not only recover the contemplative dimension of the Gospel but also rediscover our role as embodied vessels of God's *shalom* and channels of divine life between the realms of matter and spirit. I have no idea how this will happen or how many years, decades, centuries, or millennia it may be until the vision outlined here becomes the living reality for the church as a whole. In the meantime, I believe we can begin the process by developing a body practice designed to support the integration of the body in contemplative transformation. What are some of the essential components of such a practice? Among other attributes, it will:

- Be Christian. Due to the specific nature of the embodied energies cultivated, simply borrowing exercises from other traditions is not sufficient.[26]

- Include preparatory "outer" physical practices that will help shift a body from a state of habitual tension to a state of habitual relaxation and heal the nervous system.

- Support the transition from outer (self-initiated) practices to interior, effortless physical release in silent contemplative practice.

- Be rooted in Christian anthropology, understanding the human person as body, soul, and spirit in undivided unity, with the whole human person destined for eternal life.

- Engage the dynamic of fear and trust as expressed in the body as tension and relaxation. This will facilitate the development of a kinetic sense of trust in God, grounded in an open body.

- Cultivate equanimity in regard to all physical sensation, training the body and psyche not to contract in the face of pain or fear.

+ Be informed by what body-integrated practices were previously available in the Christian past. This may include Eastern Orthodox Hesychasm's integration of silent prayer with breath and heartbeat awareness[27] and the Western monastic understanding of manual labor as prayer.

+ Open the doorway to a recovery of physical healing as a central ministry of the church and a natural capacity of spiritually mature Christians.[28]

+ Cultivate both the ascent and descent aspects of body-integrated contemplation, training and preparing the body for both movements of divine Life flowing through the body.

+ Open the doorway for a deeper energetic resonance with the Transfiguration, the Crucifixion, and the Resurrection, and draw on the earthly life of Jesus as a template for the physical transformation of the serious practitioner.

Only fifty years ago, contemplation itself was virtually unheard of in Western Christianity outside of the contemplative monastic orders. Today, hundreds of thousands of people practice contemplative disciplines. I believe the day is coming, and indeed must come, when this same recovery will occur with the integration of the body in contemplative practice. May we be open to God's transforming power—spirit, soul, *and* body!

Notes

1. Thomas Keating, *Open Mind, Open Heart,* 20th ann. ed. (New York: Continuum, 2006).

2. Cynthia Bourgeault, in *The Heart of Centering Prayer* (Boulder, CO: Shambhala Publications, 2016), beautifully describes the role of the

physiological heart in contemplative Christian practice. Her book is a good starting point, as the physiological shift of "putting the mind into the heart" that she articulates is a beginning stage of bringing physiology into prayer.

3. See Francis MacNutt, *The Healing Reawakening: Reclaiming our Lost Inheritance* (Grand Rapids, MI: Chosen Books, 2006). MacNutt claims that physical healing was the primary means by which Christianity spread throughout the ancient world.

4. An ancient Chinese discipline devoted to cultivating (*gong*) internal energy/breath/essence (*qi*). For more information, see Kenneth Cohen, *The Way of Qigong: The Art and Science of Chinese Energy Healing* (New York: Ballantine, 1997), and Yap Soon-Yeong and Chok C. Hiew, *Energy Medicine in CFQ Healing: Healing the Body, Transforming Consciousness* (self-pub., 2002), iUniverse. Yap Soon-Yeong was my qigong teacher in Malaysia.

5. As an example, the fruit of "gentleness" is embodied in a nervous system that easily remains in the parasympathetic state in the face of conflict or verbal attacks.

6. *Huios anthropos* in New Testament Greek, also translated as "Son of Man" in most contemporary translations. See the vision in Daniel 7:13–14, and Jesus's reference of this text before the Sanhedrin in Matthew 26:64, Mark 14:62, Luke 22:67–70. Also note Jesus's frequent reference to himself as *huios anthropos* in the synoptic gospels. In Mark alone, this occurs nine times (2:10, 2:28, 8:38, 9:9, 9:30, 10:33, 10:45, 13:26, 14:62).

7. Genesis 1:27, 5:1–2, 9:6; Psalm 8:5–6; Wisdom 2:23; James 3:9; 1 John 3:2.

8. This integration also shatters the illusion of a dualistic separation between matter and spirit. I suspect that this ancient dualistic belief was developed by people whose lived experience was one of bodily disharmony. If so, their philosophy simply confirmed their own bodily experience of matter and spirit in conflict.

9. An essential belief of gnostic heresies, and sadly prevalent in modern Christianity.

10. On this planet, at least! There may be other species called to this same role on planets with complex life. Perhaps this is a critical point of the evolutionary process, understood theologically: to develop organisms capable of becoming a conscious link between Creator and creation throughout the universe. There are echoes of this perspective in the evolutionary theology of Pierre Teilhard de Chardin; see *The Phenomenon of Man* (New York: Harper Perennial Modern Thought, 2008).

11. For example, eating fish in Luke 24:42–43.

12. 2 Corinthians 5:17; 1 John 3:3.

13. Thomas Keating, *Invitation to Love*, 20th ann. ed. (London: Bloomsbury, 2011). Keating teaches that as we age, human emotional life is constricted by the development of a "false self" that centers around acquiring excessive fulfillment of the primary "energy centers" of security and survival, affection and esteem, and power and control. Each person develops increasingly sophisticated "emotional programs for happiness" designed to feed these perceived needs. These programs limit our emotional ability to respond freely to the experiences of everyday life.

14. This principle cannot be absolutized. It is also true that for many, serious physical disability can be a catalyst for the breakdown of the false self and profound spiritual awakening.

15. These four aspects—breathing, posture, movement, and relaxation—are the core components of Systema practice. See Konstantin Komorov, *Systema Manual* (Toronto: Systema Headquarters, 2014).

16. For example, see Fr. Keating's writing that "when the body slips away from the spirit, no great change is going to take place. In deep prayer you do not think about the body anyway. The prospect of dying is not so threatening because you have experienced a preview of what it might be like for the spirit to be separated from the body, and it is delightful." Keating, *Open Mind, Open Heart*, 53.

17. Hence Fr. Thomas's use of the term *the Divine Therapy* to describe how God heals the soul during Centering Prayer practice. See Thomas Keating, *Manifesting God* (New York: Lantern Books, 2005), 88–107.

18. When Fr. Thomas is asked a question about the healing aspect of Centering Prayer practice, "Does the healing extend to the body as well as

the soul?" Fr. Thomas replies, "Illnesses that are largely psychosomatic can certainly be healed by bringing peace to one's emotional life." Keating, *Open Mind, Open Heart,* 106. The physical effects of the prayer are described purely as an overflow of emotional healing.

19. Vladimir Vasiliev, and Scott Meredith, *Let Every Breath: Secrets of the Russian Breath Masters* (Toronto: Systema Headquarters, 2006), 123.

20. Note that all of these saints are from the second millennia of Christianity. Compare their life spans to the third-century desert contemplatives St. Anthony of Egypt (age 106) and St. Paul the Hermit (age 113). While one can argue that these exalted ages are more the result of hagiographic liberties, they fall within the range of historic human life spans, a far cry from the eight-hundred and nine-hundred year life spans depicted in Genesis 5. Interestingly, an attribution of similar long life was not given to revered urban saints of the same era. For example, Irenaeus, Ignatius of Antioch, Augustine, and Athanasius are all reported to have lived into their seventies, a ripe old age for the early centuries of the Christian era but thirty or forty years short of the great Desert Fathers and Mothers. I think there is at least the possibility that these hermit saints had attained a high level of bodily integration into their contemplative practice. On a purely physical level, recent research suggests severe calorie restriction may significantly enhance longevity (see Richard Conniff, "The Hunger Gains: Extreme Calorie-Restriction Diet Shows Anti-Aging Results," *Scientific American,* February 16, 2017, https://www.scientificamerican.com/article /the-hunger-gains-extreme-calorie-restriction-diet-shows-anti-aging -results; and Jon Gertner, "The Calorie Restriction Experiment," *New York Times,* October 7, 2009, https://www.nytimes.com/2009/10/11/ magazine/11Calories-t.html). The desert monastics were renowned for the simplicity of their diets and extensive fasting practices.

21. This has also been my personal experience. I am occasionally called by God to multiweek solo wilderness retreats. During this time, praying many hours a day, I experience a great deal of pain moving through my body, with accompanying images and awareness of others' suffering. If I stay in a state of body awareness, the pain "passes through" both consciousness and body awareness without leaving physiological damage. When I do not tend to my body in a retreat like this, I can

quickly become ill or debilitated, something I learned through hard experience.

22. What flows from this is an ideal of a body that is simultaneously whole (integrated) in itself and interconnected with the suffering of others. This is quite different from the modern Western ideal of physical perfection in body form, separated from any suffering, illness, or disease in itself or others.

23. Thomas Keating writes: "Empirical evidence seems to be growing that the consequences of traumatic emotional experiences from earliest childhood are stored in our bodies and nervous systems in the form of tension, anxiety, and various defense mechanisms. Ordinary rest and sleep do not get rid of them. But with interior silence and the profound rest that this brings to the whole organism, these emotional blocks begin to soften up, and the natural capacity of the human organism to throw off things that are harmful starts to evacuate them. The psyche as well as the body has its way of evacuating material that is harmful to its health. The emotional residue in our unconscious emerges during prayer in the form of thoughts have a certain urgency, energy, and emotional charge to them. Keating, *Open Mind, Open Heart*, 95. I would add that with physical preparation, the residue Fr. Keating speaks of can also be released in the form of heat, cold, trembling, and tingling sensations in bodily tissues. I have found when bodily release is included in the purification process, there is a decreased intensity of compulsive thoughts, charged emotions, and mental imagery. It is as if the blockages can be released along multiple pathways, and when released bodily they do not express as strongly in the emotional and mental realms.

24. I don't theologically believe in a "heaven is up, earth is below" worldview, but there is an unmistakable felt sense of these directions in the experiences I am attempting to describe here.

25. I do not mean this as merely a poetic metaphor! People in this state literally take in some part of the suffering and disunity of the world and let it flow through their bodies into unity in God.

26. Some of my universalizing colleagues may cringe at this statement. But this has become very clear to me as an objective truth over the course of twenty years and more than ten thousand hours of working with

subtle energies. Each practice bears a particular energetic imprint on the body, and they are not identical. There are philosophical *themes* and *principles* that may be universal across practices, but the specific energetic impacts of the practice are unique. Trying to develop the energetic pathways of multiple schools of cultivation at the same time can inhibit progress in any of them.

27. For examples of breath and heart prayer in the Orthodox tradition, see Gregory Palamas's fourteenth-century text *Triads in Defense of the Holy Hesychasts*, trans. Nicholas Gendle (Mahwah, NJ: Paulist Press, 1983); and the anonymous nineteenth-century Russian classic *The Way of a Pilgrim*, trans. R. M. French (San Francisco: HarperSanFrancisco, 1984).

28. Integrated, healed bodies naturally have the ability to transmit aspects of the state of wholeness to others. Physical healing can often be understood as a natural, not merely supernatural or miraculous, aspect of Christian faith.

Beatrice Bruteau: Prophet of a New Revelation

MATTHEW WRIGHT

> *A new revelation is coming, and many threads from the past will be woven into it, drawn from all the old traditions. But some of the "former things" will "pass away" (Rev 21:4)—whatever is incompatible with planetary peaceful life together.*
>
> —Beatrice Bruteau[1]

One of the most profound thinkers and visionaries of this past century's Christian contemplative reawakening was the late Dr. Beatrice Bruteau. Bruteau was an interspiritual pioneer, working at the intersections of Vedanta and Christian mysticism, and a student (and further elaborator) of the evolutionary thought of Pierre Teilhard de Chardin and Sri Aurobindo Ghose. She founded Schola Contemplatonis, a network for contemplatives, and authored twelve books on Christian and interspiritual thought. She died quietly on November 16, 2014.

Bruteau was convinced that humanity stands on the cusp of something new: a new way of understanding religion and spirituality, a new way of understanding the universe, and, perhaps most importantly, a new way of understanding our place and our role within the unfolding drama of cosmic history. She called this emerging vision "a new revelation." She wrote, "We will need stories even about how this new thing has arisen and what it means. But those stories will come. The time of revelation is not past. Revelation is what the whole history of the world is."[2]

She was a prophet of the new revelation, weaving its threads together throughout her writings and in her life. While less known than her male colleagues—figures such as Thomas Merton and Thomas Keating—Bruteau was often more daring in her thought, and she remains a significant voice in laying the groundwork for an integrative twenty-first-century contemplative vision, big enough to embrace threads ranging from evolutionary thought and nonduality to pluralism and social justice. I first became aware of her work at the recommendation of my own mentor, contemplative teacher and Episcopal priest Cynthia Bourgeault. Bourgeault says that when she encountered Bruteau's work in the 1980s, her "spiritual universe [was] quietly but completely overturned. Correspondence soon led to a personal visit and a mentoring relationship that would span the next three decades."[3]

An Evolutionary Vision

For Bruteau, the first and most significant thread of the new revelation—the linchpin—was a dynamic, evolutionary vision of God and cosmos. "A theology of evolution," she writes, "sees God as deeply involved in the evolutionary process of the world. God is making the world by means of evolution. And the evolutionary process in its turn is seen as striving toward God." More than that, "God is Self-expressing and

Self-realizing in evolution."[4] This dynamic reciprocity—the world unfolding from and toward God, and God unfolding in and through the world—represents a quantum leap that leaves us in an entirely different theological ballpark from the one most of us have learned to play in.

Bruteau tied this vision to the Christian doctrine of the Incarnation—understood not simply as God taking flesh once alone in Jesus of Nazareth but as "the real presence of the Creator in and even as the created, extending the Christology familiar to trinitarians to the entire cosmos."[5] For Bruteau, the Incarnation of God was a cosmic and unending event, unfolding through (and as) the entire evolutionary process: "Life itself is God in each of us, pursuing the endless task of the Incarnation."[6] This dynamic, open-ended vision replaces the more fixed and static views of history and creation often found in traditional religious systems.

While many religious traditions in the modern world have grown comfortable with the basic evolutionary map, there's a tendency to see it simply as a replacement creation narrative; with the emergence of human beings, the earlier, static (or, alternatively, degenerative) map of reality returns. Bruteau wasn't satisfied with this picture. Summarizing the vision of the French Jesuit and paleontologist Pierre Teilhard de Chardin, she writes, "It is because we can look back and see the pattern, see it recurring, that Teilhard believed we can legitimately extrapolate and project the pattern into the future, looking forward to another creative union in which *we* will be the uniting elements."[7] In other words, evolution is not over.

Just as subatomic particles, atoms, and molecules before us united in "creative unions" that opened new evolutionary playing fields, so too human beings are potentially the building blocks that can unite to form a new evolutionary leap. Taking a planetary view of the evolutionary process, Teilhard charted three major stages within the wider unfolding: the emergence of a *geosphere* (the planet itself), a *biosphere* (a layer of organic life around the surface of the planet), and finally a *noosphere* (from the Greek *nous*, or mind)—a sphere of conscious awareness that in humanity has become uniquely self-reflexive. Looking forward then, the next evolutionary leap will not happen primarily where we're accustomed to looking for evolution—in the biosphere—but instead, following the pattern that has already unfolded, in the next rung up the evolutionary ladder: in the noosphere, in human consciousness. Bruteau explains:

> In order for us as human beings to unite with one another to form the next creative union, according to the same pattern that the atoms and molecules and cells followed before us, we must share with one another our characteristic energies. . . . And what is human energy? It is not just physical energy or chemical energy or biological energy. It is the energy of thinking, or knowing, and the energy of loving, or willing. It is this most intimate energy of ours that we are asked to commit to the new union.[8]

She believed that human beings, united in knowledge, love, and will, would form the new higher-level collectivity that will itself be the next evolutionary arising: "We are being asked to give ourselves *as persons* in order to create a higher-level New Being."[9] This new arising will not happen automatically, however, as it will require something never before needed at previous evolutionary junctures: humanity's conscious will to form a new, higher union:

> At this point, evolution meets a situation that is unique in its history: the uniting elements, in our case, are free agents. We will not automatically unite merely because of some natural affinity. Since each of us is free, we can each choose whether we will enter into the proposed union or not. . . . This is why Teilhard says that the whole cosmic enterprise now hangs on our decision: *we are evolution*.[10]

Humanity must choose to unite in knowledge, love, and will to carry the process forward. Teilhard hopefully prophesied: "The day will come when, after harnessing space, the winds, the tides, and gravitation, we shall harness for God the energies of love. And, on that day, for the second time in the history of the world, human beings will have discovered fire."[11] If that day is to come, however, humanity's conscious effort will be necessary.

The Significance of Practice

With Teilhard, Bruteau saw that love alone can produce the atmosphere in which the new union will emerge—if it is to emerge at all. But how do we cultivate this kind of love? Bruteau believed contemplative practice held the key, contributing the practical how-to of this next, unprecedented evolutionary leap. Love in its higher, more altruistic forms is essentially a nonegocentric expression of energy—it flows out beyond the limited self without seeking anything in return. Humanity's current energy patterns, however, are largely egocentric—concerned only for the individual self, or for those of our own tribal (national, ethnic, religious) affiliations. Bruteau saw the need for the rerouting of our essential human energies if we are to evolve:

If we are to make this change in favor of forming a New Being, we will have to redirect our energy currents. And it will take energy even to make that option. You see, our energy currents are egocentric— the currents flow out from the ego, grasp what's good for the ego, and flow back to the ego. This energy pattern cannot form a creative union because it tries to assimilate all other beings to the being of the ego.[12]

We need a way of opening our human faculties to new, nonegocentric patterns of energy flow. Bruteau saw that this was the essential work of all contemplative practice: to aid the individual in dis-identifying with our usual, limited constructions of selfhood, which keep our characteristic human energies caught in the egocentric feedback loop. We must realize what she termed *deep self*: "The deep self is not defined, not described by any of the qualities of our bodies or personalities, by our histories or social positions, our jobs, or our religions."[13] That is, the deep self is not identified with any of the boundaries we use to reinforce egoic and tribal division, which in turn prevent the arising of a higher collectivity.

Spiritual practice is central to this realization: "This depth is currently buried and hidden in most of us. Yet, we also sense that it is there, waiting to be brought into full presence, and so we do various spiritual practices in the hope of becoming fully aware of our deep reality."[14] Contemplative practice cultivates non-identified presence, breaking the egocentric feedback loop and freeing our characteristic human energy in such a way that it can be shared in a new creative union, beyond the boundaries that currently divide us—from one another, from the earth, from God.

The linking of contemplative practice and spiritual discipline with our potential to further the evolution of consciousness has gained traction in recent years within the field of neuroscience. Just as Teilhard worked to uncover the history of evolution within the layers of the earth, neuroscientists have uncovered a similar record within the layers of the human brain. Cynthia Bourgeault has summed up this cerebrological dig nicely:

> It is by now well known that the human brain is actually four-brains-in-one, built up sequentially over ten thousand years or more of evolution. Our primitive hindbrain (sometimes called our "reptilian brain") we share with our animal ancestors, and as with all animal brains, its primary concerns are the tasks of survival and self-defense. On top of and surrounding this ancient brain, nature has gradually built up three additional brains: the "old mammalian" or emotional-cognitive brain, the seat of our emotional intelligence; the neo-cortex, with its capacities for complex and creative thinking; and the prefrontal lobes, with their overall harmonizing and integrating effect.[15]

So how does this relate to contemplative practice? In just this way: *contemplative practice reroutes our neural pathways*. To quote Bourgeault again, "What neuroscience has been able to confirm is that any initial negative response to an outside stimulus immediately activates the reptilian brain, with its highly energized but extremely limited and archaic defensive maneuvers."[16] In other words, inner gestures of fear and negativity immediately throw us back into the least-evolved center of our brain. This "reptilian brain" governs fight-or-flight responses and keeps us locked in a primarily dualistic, either/or mode of thinking. This, of course, is the mode of consciousness that gives rise to egocentrism and tribalism, short-circuiting the possibility of the next creative union.

Contemplative spiritual disciplines, on the other hand, work to access "deep self," creating an inner spaciousness within human awareness that reroutes our neural pathways toward the more highly evolved sectors of the brain. As we act increasingly from these more developed centers of intelligence, rather than the more dualistic and fear-based, we lay down stronger neural pathways in the direction needed to make creative union possible at the next level. Put simply, contemplative practice evolves our brain.

Complexified Nonduality

For Bruteau, the spiritual realization to which both contemplative practice and the evolution of consciousness are wending is *nondual*, a term derived from the Sanskrit *advaita*, which literally means "not-two." A nondual vision sees no ultimate separation between God and creation, self and other, or self and God, but instead a dynamic, unified whole. Over time, contemplative practice anchors this "seeing from oneness" as a new and increasingly dominant mode of human perception.

Bruteau recognized a tendency, however, in certain traditional nondual systems—expressions of Advaita Vedanta, for example—to privilege or prioritize the "absolute" or "unmanifest" dimensions of reality over "the relative" or "manifest." In such a system, both the material world and the individuated self can be seen as "traps" or "illusions" that are ultimately to be seen through or escaped. Resisting

this impulse, Bruteau named her nondual vision "complexified nonduality," which Cynthia Bourgeault succinctly summarizes as "not one, not two, but both one and two."[17] In
Bruteau's words,

> It's a nondualism that doesn't reduce to a monism.
> That is to say, our personal energies do not *merge*
> or become *submerged* in some amorphous whole.
> We do not acquire a kind of oceanic sense of being
> swallowed up in a great All. Quite the contrary: sub-
> jectively, it feels rather like an *intensification* of indi-
> viduality—Self-consciousness or Self-realization.[18]

Bruteau's insight remains true to Teilhard's fundamental dic-
tum, "Union differentiates."[19] Looking at each creative union
within the evolutionary process, Teilhard saw that when elements unite, they are not dissolved into one another—atoms
are not lost in a new unit called a molecule. Instead, their
individuality is caught up in a more complex, *more* differentiated reality. The more that elements unite, the more complex,
differentiated, and diversified reality becomes. He resisted
any system that looked "backward" to an undifferentiated,
primordial unity—and was sometimes simplistically critical
of certain Eastern contemplative traditions because of this.

Teilhard, however, was looking primarily in one direction: forward and outward, toward becoming. What Bruteau realized was that the interior movement, characteristic
of contemplative spirituality, toward the realization of "deep
self"—that which is dis-identified from differentiated form—
is utterly and somewhat counterintuitively essential, not
counter, to the forward movement of becoming. Because, she
maintained, when you discover deep self, "you discover that
its intention is toward becoming."

The deep Self in you is the Absolute, the Infinite, the Eternal, the Divine, and it's manifesting as the particular human being that you're embodied as, at the present time. So I would say there are two poles. There is a mystical pole, which is what Shankara [the founder of Advaita Vedanta] invites us to, and then there is the creative pole, which is this whole evolutionary movement.[20]

What Bruteau here terms the *mystical* and *creative* poles of our being are roughly synonymous with being/becoming, contemplation/evolution, and unmanifest/manifest. Each pole is essential and fundamental, and significantly they are *not* contrary or contradictory movements, as our spiritual traditions have often imagined, but complementary and mutually implicating.

For Bruteau, the drive of "deep self" or the "unmanifest" is always *toward* becoming, *toward* manifestation—otherwise there would be no world. And so it follows that "a nondualism that eventually rejects or escapes the whole domain of manifestation deprives the process of its own intrinsic value."[21] The more we realize our nondual identity with this ultimate Self, the more we open ourselves to the evolutionary movement of becoming. Ultimately, each vision serves and is completed by the other.

Complex nondualism urges that we do not need to reject the manifest phase in order to perfect the unmanifest phase. Rather, the desired position is to rest in the Unmanifest and express in the Manifest, not alternately but simultaneously and by mutual implication. The Unmanifest, being of the nature of agape, necessarily radiates Being, thus expressing as

Manifest. And the Manifest, realizing its deep nature *as* the expression of the Unmanifest, experiences itself as That.[22]

For Bruteau, such a vision was at the heart of Christian spirituality's "incarnational" road map—what she labeled "cosmic incarnational mysticism"—a full-on embrace of phenomenal existence that sees the world as "the Body of God."[23] In such a system, any scheme that necessitates a final rejection of the manifest sets up an inherent duality and therefore cannot be accurately called nondual. Manifest and Unmanifest are one, not in the overcoming of one by the other, but in each finding in the other its own fulfilment. "Our evolution in consciousness," Bruteau said, "is aimed at this complex Self-realization and enlightenment. Our spiritual practices are to bring us to that realization."[24]

Bruteau's complexified nonduality leaves us with a contemplative vision that is fully engaged with life in the world. There is no bifurcation or contradiction between "active" and "contemplative" vocations, between the social reformer and the mystic. For Bruteau, the activist's vision of a transformed world is *fueled* by the discovery of deep self, and it is only *from* deep self that authentic societal transformation can ultimately emerge. "Such a mysticism," she wrote,

> will manifest itself not in withdrawal from the world and understanding of the world, but in realization of the Transcendent Reality precisely in the movements of the world—physical, chemical, biological, social, scientific, political, artistic, religious—and in active, intelligent, compassionate, responsible, beautiful, happy *working with* these dimensions.[25]

Contemplation, then, can never be an escape from the world, but is always preparation for a full and free engagement with the whole of life.

The Future of Religion

It's obvious that spiritual practice is essential to Bruteau's vision, but what of religion? Many are the voices that claim our existing religious forms are outdated and incongruent with our emerging consciousness; to borrow a metaphor from Jesus: new wine requires new wineskins. Bruteau, however, was not so quick to make this leap. For her, the existing religions cannot so easily be chocked up to "old wineskins" and chucked out, but are themselves evolving realities. And, as with humanity, there is no reason they could not go right on evolving.

As she notes, however, in the quotation that opened this chapter, while the new revelation will be "drawn from all the old traditions," "some of the 'former things' will 'pass away' (Rev 21:4)—whatever is incompatible with planetary peaceful life together."[26] And so, a more apt metaphor for religious evolution than wineskins might be tree growth: as a tree expands year by year to express new and larger life, the old, constricting layer of bark—once the tree's protection at an earlier stage of development—is pushed off and a new layer emerges (until it, too, becomes too confining). Those elements of religion that promote tribalism—superiority complexes and theological exclusivity—will need to fall away like old bark, but nothing of each tradition's vital life will be lost.

Bruteau rejected outright any system in which a single religion became the "umbrella" under which all others must be arranged (or rejected). Here, she went beyond her teacher

Teilhard de Chardin, who for all his cosmic inclusivity still saw Judaism as superseded by Christianity, and Islam worthy of little attention because, in his own words,

> in spite of the number of its adherents and its continual progress (in the less evolved strata of mankind, we may note) . . . it contributes no special solution to the modern religious problem. It seems to me to represent a residual Judaism, with no individual character of its own, and it can develop only by becoming either humanist or Christian.[27]

This strand of Teilhard's thought is no doubt shocking and embarrassing to the contemporary interspiritually sensitive seeker, and in a more interspiritual climate he might have found in these traditions, particularly in the mystical frameworks of Jewish Kabbalah and Islamic Sufism, spiritualties deeply congruent with his own world-affirming and evolutionary approach. Rebuffing Teilhard on this point, and drawing on contemporary ecological models that see all life as interconnected and interdependent, Bruteau writes,

> Taking a privileged viewpoint—choosing one traditional spirituality to be the umbrella, or the master form, for the planetary soul—is not an ecological way of proceeding. The ecological paradigm shows all parties collaborating with equal dignity and constituting jointly the "we" of the ecosystem.[28]

By separating Teilhard's evolutionary mysticism from an inherently Christian framework, she revealed it as a potentially reorienting ground for all religions, rather than the umbrella that gave one an advantage over the others. Her incarnational and evolutionary approach also allows for a significant reframing: our spiritual traditions need no longer be seen as competing paths of "ascent" or "return" to God (we've never left) but mutually enriching paths flowing *out* from God, as God flows ever more fully into form, expression, and Self-realization—through and as life itself.[29]

Following Teilhard, Bruteau saw that in our global era we are entering a vast process of convergence. Human evolution initially unfolded along the opposite trajectory: divergence. As our species fanned out around the globe, we developed along different lines of ethnic, cultural, linguistic, and religious evolution. As we now enter an era of global interconnection—thanks largely to developments in technology and transportation—divergence is coming to an end.

Around the globe, our various cultures, languages, ethnicities, and religions are converging. Bruteau points out what is now obvious: "When we get off the planet, as the astronauts and cosmonauts did, we can see that there are no boundaries marking out the ranges of nations, or races, or religions." How will religion function in a boundary-less world? Bruteau predicted what we are increasingly seeing: religious hybridization:

> Different approaches to spirituality have developed among the diverse peoples of the Earth in the same way that variants and distinct species have developed biologically: by separation. Each tribal unit had its own representation of deity and its own customs. But when these separations are overcome, then sharing takes over more and more—even while conflicts are still going on—and hybrids begin to appear.[30]

More than ever, we see Christians who practice yoga, Jews committed to Buddhist meditation, children raised in interfaith homes. Old lines of division are no longer holding. "It is going to be harder and harder," Bruteau wrote, "to preserve the doctrinal and ritual purity of particular spiritualities in a world that is becoming so intimately interconnected."[31] The question, of course, is, is this a problem?

While we often think of our religious traditions as bounded and unchanging, and hear voices of interfaith dialogue that are quick to cry out against the dangers of "syncretism," Bruteau pointed out that our religions have been mixing and mingling from the get-go:

> The Jews were influenced by their neighbors, and the materials we have in the Bible represent gatherings from Egypt, Babylonia, and Persia, as well as Hebrew experiences. Christianity grew out of Judaism but was heavily influenced by Greek philosophy, Roman polity, and maybe even Hindu spirituality. The Western church adopted first Platonic and, later, quite different Aristotelian philosophical concepts, and each time declared them to be orthodox teaching. Look at what happened to Buddhism in China, when it intermarried with Taoism, and later in Japan where it was adapted to fit the indigenous culture. Islam acknowledges that it has built its house on Jewish and Christian foundations. And Hinduism simply absorbs every spiritual nutrient set before it and assimilates it into its own identity.[32]

Our religions have never been static, isolated, or monolithic realities; they have always been evolving organisms, as they continue to be. The truth, of course, is that just as we *are* evolution, we *are* our religions. They do not exist as abstractions apart from the human beings and communities that embody them. As *we* evolve, religion will evolve. As *we* cultivate friendships and marriages and families across old lines of division and conflict, our religions will do likewise. And while this process of linking and bridging traditions can be done in more or less thoughtful and skillful ways, the process cannot be reversed.

The ultimate question, Bruteau felt, was:

> [W]hat shall we mean when we say "we"? What is the scope of the context? Where do we position the horizon of our domain? In particular, if—let us say—Catholics can draw from Benedictine, Franciscan, Dominican, and Carmelite sources without feeling that they have gone outside the borders of their appropriate "we," why cannot all of us expand those borders? Why can we not, as human beings, draw from all the traditions on Earth? The question is: How big is our "we"?[33]

Seen in planetary perspective, our religions become not lines of division but the shared spiritual resources of the entire human family. And this is why our existing great religions continue to be important—they are the primary bearers and preservers of the spiritual practices and disciplines that best facilitate the evolution of human consciousness. These spiritual technologies do the work of rerouting our neural pathways toward greater compassion, inclusivity, and creative intelligence. Our religions contain the stories, practices, and devotional focal points that can set our hearts on fire with love and ready us to give ourselves to one another in the next creative union.

Bruteau saw our need for religion, but she also saw the danger: Does our religious framework and practice free or constrict our consciousness? She insisted that when we use the language and concepts of any tradition,

what we say by means of this language should be . . .
that the sacred concepts, doctrines, images, practices
of this tradition themselves point beyond any exclusivist claim for themselves. Every "world-class" spiritual
tradition has a way of talking about universal unity.[34]

For those of us who practice or serve within a religious tradition, our work is to reorient that tradition toward the most
unitive vision to which our sacraments and sacred metaphors
can point us. Only in this way can the blessings of our lineages flow forward into, and serve, the future. Can we offer
up our sacred stories, practices, and disciplines as so many
threads in a new revelation? If so, Bruteau believed, we could
come together in singing a new song, woven together from
the music of all our traditions.

Why should any of us insist that our particular his-
tory/doctrine/practice is the major theme, the melody,
to which others can be considered harmony, counter-
point, accompaniment, back-up group? Why should
we not each sing our own melodic line, interweaving
it with all others so that the whole composes a living, moving harmony? Why not be a jazz band and
improvise, with each musical creating—within the
general, the generic, universal, planetary themes—a
unique contribution? Why not all the Earth pray a
polyphonic prayer?[35]

We Are the Revolution

Beatrice Bruteau beautifully wove together the music of
evolution, nonduality, contemplative practice, and religious

pluralism into a polyphonic prayer on behalf of the world's becoming, leaving us with a vision of a possible future: a future only we can create. She told a story of God incarnate, God manifesting and realizing Godself through the cosmos, through you and me. It's a profoundly hopeful story, and one big enough to hold all of the stories that came before—a story in which the world matters, our religions matter, and we matter.

It's also a story that asks something of us: Can we relinquish something of our imagined autonomy and independence, our limiting identities, borders, and boundaries, to form a new higher-order collectivity—a new "we"—the likes of which our species has never seen before? This emerging, faintly glimpsed "we" is the ground of the new arising. Our "we" is perhaps the New Being itself. We do not need to leave our religions behind to see its arrival, and, indeed, perhaps we can't get there without them. We don't need to lose our individuality in a monistic sea of unity to realize the divine life, but only to add it to the building up of a New Being, a growing collectivity—to the ever-deepening disclosure of God's life-in-form.

The last words I leave to our storyteller and prophet:

> We cannot wait for the world to turn, for the times to change that we may change with them, for the revolution to come and carry us round in its new course. No more will the evolutionary forces of nature propel us in their groping way through the next critical point into a new state of Being. From now on, if we are to have any future, *we must create that future ourselves.* We ourselves are the future and we are the revolution.[36]

Notes

1. Beatrice Bruteau, "Eucharistic Ecology and Ecological Spirituality," *Cross Currents* 40, no. 4 (Winter 90–91): 499, http://www.crosscurrents .org/eucharist.htm.

2. Bruteau, "Eucharistic Ecology and Ecological Spirituality."

3. Cynthia Bourgeault, "A Tribute to Beatrice Bruteau." https:// www.contemplative.org/a-tribute-to-beatrice-bruteau-by -cynthia-bourgeault/

4. Beatrice Bruteau, "A Song that Goes on Singing," interview by Amy Edelstein and Ellen Daly, *What Is Enlightenment?* (Spring–Summer 2002).

5. Beatrice Bruteau, *God's Ecstasy: The Creation of a Self-Creating World* (New York: Crossroad, 1997), 21.

6. Beatrice Bruteau, *Evolution toward Divinity: Teilhard de Chardin and the Hindu Traditions* (Wheaton, IL: Theosophical Publishing House, 1974), 26.

7. Bruteau, "A Song that Goes on Singing."

8. Bruteau, "A Song that Goes on Singing."

9. Bruteau, "A Song that Goes on Singing."

10. Bruteau, "A Song that Goes on Singing."

11. Kevin F. Burke, Eileen Burke-Sullivan, Phyllis Zagano, eds., *The Ignatian Tradition: Spirituality in History* (Collegeville, MN: Liturgical Press, 2009), 86.

12. Bruteau. "A Song that Goes on Singing."

13. Bruteau. "A Song that Goes on Singing."

14. Bruteau. "A Song that Goes on Singing."

15. Cynthia Bourgeault, *The Wisdom Jesus: Transforming Heart and Mind—a New Perspective on Christ and His Message* (Boston: Shambhala Publications, 2008), 175–76.

16. Bourgeault, *Wisdom Jesus*, 176.

17. Cynthia Bourgeault, *The Meaning of Mary Magdalene: Discovering the Woman at the Heart of Christianity* (Boston: Shambhala Publications, 2010), 134.

18. Bruteau, "A Song that Goes on Singing."

19. Blanche Gallagher, *Meditations with Teilhard de Chardin* (Rochester, VT: Bear & Company, 1988).

20. Bruteau, "A Song that Goes on Singing."

21. Bruteau, "A Song that Goes on Singing."

22. Bruteau, "A Song that Goes on Singing."

23. Bruteau, *God's Ecstasy*, 176–78.

24. Bruteau, "A Song that Goes on Singing."

25. Bruteau, *God's Ecstasy*, 178.

26. Bruteau, "Eucharistic Ecology and Ecological Spirituality."

27. Bruteau, "Eucharistic Ecology and Ecological Spirituality."

28. Bruteau, "Eucharistic Ecology and Ecological Spirituality."

29. I first heard this particular insight and framing from Cynthia Bourgeault.

30. Bruteau, "Eucharistic Ecology and Ecological Spirituality."

31. Bruteau, "Eucharistic Ecology and Ecological Spirituality."

32. Bruteau, "Eucharistic Ecology and Ecological Spirituality."

33. Bruteau, "Eucharistic Ecology and Ecological Spirituality."

34. Bruteau, "Eucharistic Ecology and Ecological Spirituality."

35. Bruteau, "Eucharistic Ecology and Ecological Spirituality."

36. Bruteau, "A Song that Goes on Singing."

Afterword

MARGARET BENEFIEL

Fifty years ago, the Spirit stirred Thomas Keating, Tilden Edwards, Richard Rohr, and Laurence Freeman toward a rediscovery of contemplative prayer in the West. While Eastern forms of meditation had begun to come to the West, these contemplative explorers discovered, each in his own way, that his own Christian tradition contained a contemplative core. They began to spread this message and to invite others to join them in contemplative practice. Their individual journeys led to the creation of three major Christian contemplative organizations: Keating, Contemplative Outreach; Edwards, the Shalem Institute for Spiritual Formation; Rohr, the Center for Action and Contemplation; and Freeman (following John Main), the World Community for Christian Meditation.

At the initiative of Keating, the founders of these organizations met with him in early October 2016 at St. Benedict's Monastery in Snowmass, Colorado. Subsequently, the executive directors and appointed representatives of their respective organizations met later that month in Washington, DC: Gail Fitzpatrick-Hopler and Mary Ann Best, Contemplative Outreach; Margaret Benefiel, Shalem Institute; Michael Poffenberger, Center for Action and Contemplation; and Dennis McAuliffe, World Community for Christian Meditation.

These meetings focused on deepening friendships and explored the possibility of collaboration in furthering the contemplative awakening in the world today. The statement that came out of the second meeting, which includes the statement from the first meeting, follows:

> On October 5–8, 2016, our founders met and released the following statement:
>
>> In October of 2016, we met in Snowmass, Colorado, to deepen our friendship and to gather and nurture a communion of Christian contemplatives. In order of age, Thomas Keating, Tilden Edwards, Richard Rohr, and Laurence Freeman are united in our commitment to renewing the practices of the Christian contemplative tradition as the center of all forms of Christian life.
>>
>> This communion is open to collaboration with all streams of contemplative wisdom in response to the urgent social needs of our time.
>>
>> In the immediate future, we look forward to encouraging dialogue with and among young Christian contemplatives in particular.
>
> On October 19–20, 2016, when the directors and appointed representatives of each founder's organization met in Washington, DC, we affirmed our founders' statement and mirrored their own deepening friendship with a commitment to deepen ties among all of our organizations in our shared mission to support the awakening of the Christian contemplative tradition. We acknowledged a common desire for greater inclusivity and diversity of experience within our communities.

The founders felt the time had come for them to support young contemplative leaders, who, like themselves fifty years ago, are experiencing fresh winds of the Spirit for our time.

As a first step, the founders invited a group of sixteen young contemplative thought leaders to meet with them in Colorado the following August to share their views, concerns, and hopes for the contemplative movement in the world today.

I was honored to have been invited to facilitate this gathering in August 2017. We gathered to notice and name the Spirit's movement. We celebrated what God has done in the renewal of contemplative prayer in the past fifty years. We celebrated what God is doing now.

Based on the premise that contemplative practice serves as the vital grounding of Christian life and service, the gathering explored how prayer moves us to respond to the urgent social and spiritual needs of our time. We grounded our time together in prayer, seeking to explore our questions through a heart-centered approach, listening for God's voice in the midst of our conversations. We took time for silence as needed, seeking to go deeper in our listening. Above all, we were willing to let go of our own agendas in order to hear and respond to God.

One of the first themes that surfaced was societal impasse. In the midst of the idyllic setting of St. Benedict's Monastery, participants remained keenly aware of the needs of the wider world and drew on Constance FitzGerald's work, "Impasse and Dark Night," to begin to make sense of the turbulence of these times and to see how God was working in the midst. One of the participants grew up in Charlottesville and carried the weight of the violent racism that had wounded her city just two days before. Others' experiences included working with homeless youth in New York, with human trafficking in

Africa, and with healing the earth from environmental devastation, to name just a few. No strangers to human suffering, these young leaders sought solid grounding for strength to face the troubled world they inherited.

Constance FitzGerald provided that solid grounding. She maintains that, while St. John of the Cross articulated the experience of impasse and dark night for individuals, the same process applies to society. On an individual level, when we are certain of ourselves and our prayer is "working," we easily slip into the illusion of control. When things fall apart and we can't see God, God is at work in the darkness, doing deeper work. On the societal level, too, FitzGerald argues, it's when things fall apart and we experience impasse that we are brought to our knees, invited to trust that God is doing deeper work than we can see. All is obscured, yet God has not departed. In fact, something more profound than we can imagine is occurring and will be revealed only in due time, like the birth that follows the darkness of gestation.

Turning to St. John of the Cross and FitzGerald for hope provided these young leaders, and can provide us, with a foundation for facing the seemingly impossible challenges that face us. We live in times that bring us to our knees. Any illusion of control over the events that surround us has slipped away. This is a time for contemplatives. We must practice living from the heart even as our hearts are breaking, as we face the racism, war, refugee crises, gun violence, political divisiveness, environmental degradation and its accompanying natural disasters, and more, that surround us.

Because God is at work, we can live in the darkness. Because we can trust that God's work is deeper than what we see or understand, we can take the next step. Because God is God, the deep mystery beyond human understanding, we can live with open hearts and confidence that good will come of our faithfulness, even when we can't see the path before us.[1]

Notes

1. The Afterword contains excerpts from two Shalem blogs (Shalem.org), used with permission: Margaret Benefiel, "Contemplative Collaboration," Shalem Institute for Spiritual Formation (blog), November 2, 2016, https://shalem.org/2016/11/02/contemplative-collaboration; and Margaret Benefiel, "Glimpsing God in the Dark Night," Shalem Institute for Spiritual Formation (blog), December 12, 2017, https://shalem.org/2017/12/06/glimpsing-god-in-the-dark-night.

Acknowledgments

Jessie and Stuart would first like to thank the entire team who helped nurture and share in the New Contemplative Leaders Exchange in Snowmass, Colorado, in August 2017. We give thanks for the insight, discernment, and humility of Tilden Edwards, Laurence Freeman, Richard Rohr, and Thomas Keating. The spaciousness of these souls enabled our own fledgling roots to search for those deep spaces that give life to our souls. We also give thanks for Margaret Benefiel, for her leadership in organizing, fundraising, and supporting the gathering, and whose compassionate presence helped hold the many stories, dreams, wonders, and questions we each brought with us into that sacred place. We also give thanks for Erik Keeney, whose novitiate at St. Benedict's Monastery was filled with the myriad details for dreaming this gathering into being. Your keen eye and kind heart held us every step of the way. As well, we deeply thank Martha Bolinger and the Trust for the Meditation Process, whose funding enabled the gathering to take place. Their generosity and vision supported us all as we traveled from all over the world to share together.

From Jessie

Mom and Dad, your love and support as parents is unmatched. Thank you for nurturing me, for caring about me, and loving me just as I am.

To my sister, Erin, and the Rittenhouse family, your listening ear, your playful love, and your hospitality are a rare and precious witness to love in the world.

Margaret Benefiel, you have been a teacher, a mentor, and someone who believed in me even when I didn't. This book would never have happened without your vision and encouragement.

Stuart, my goodness, I don't believe this project would have ever made it to the finish line without you, my friend. Thank you for being who you are. Your love for contemplative living (and chocolate!) is evident in all that you do.

Susan Henry-Crowe, thank you for your generous heart and desire for justice in the world. Your unwavering prayer and assurance that God is "working for good every day in the world" and consequent hopeful spirit is a gift to all who meet you.

To the General Board of Church and Society, you never cease to surprise me with your hope and determination for a better world.

To the Shalem community, you are a witness to Presence in the world and a constant source of inspiration for me. Thank you for teaching and practicing the practice of deep listening for where the Spirit is leading in each and every moment and in each and every life.

From Stuart

From the first time I opened Richard Foster's *Celebration of Discipline* and read his prayer that there may be more "deep people," my heart has yearned for a deeper contemplative practice. From those early days, Spirit has nurtured my own struggling prayer with elders and teachers whose support has been invaluable.

Julie Johnson and CeCe Balboni, my heart is forever grateful for your friendship and counsel. I love you dearly.

Barbara Luhn, your spiritual guidance and shared love of conversation and French fries at The Copper Pot has meant so much to me.

Julia Gatta and Martin Smith, your presence and insight helped hone not only my thesis but also my vocation.

My heart swells with gratitude to be able to serve at Grace Episcopal Church, with my staff colleagues in whose lives I see the diversity and richness of God. To Reba Page, Brenda Morgan, Will Gotmer, Jennifer Williams, Jeremy Landers, Cheryl Kelley, Liz Howington, and Ansley Forrester, to share this space with you has been an honor and a privilege.

Brian Sullivan, Sharon Hiers, and Sarah Fisher, I thank you so much for your eyes and your hearts as you supported me through drafts of my chapter. You are incredible priests, but more than that, you are amazing human beings.

Barbara Brown Taylor and Lerita Coleman Brown, you are sages and incredible teachers. I am extraordinarily grateful for you both.

Jason Voyles, your friendship and counsel has meant the world to me as I learn more and more that leading is serving and serving is full of joy.

Cynthia Park, to be a priest alongside you is a true gift from God. Thank you for the gift that is you, a being of wisdom and grace.

Jessie Smith, to share this journey with you has been a gift! I give thanks to God that our lives have connected. I also give thanks for the video conferences that enabled us to see each other's faces and laugh out loud.

Finally, to Lisa and Evelyn, my wife and daughter, you show me each day that I am loved even as you let me love you. There are no words.

~

Roy Carlisle, your early vision around this volume helped us take threads of ideas and begin weaving them into something resembling coherent thoughts. Thank you.

To Gwendolin Herder, Dan White, Emily Wichland, Tim Holtz, and the entire team at Crossroad Publishing Company, who worked long hours to shepherd this project, you are wizards of words! Thank you deeply for all you do.

Bibliography

Bachelard, Sarah. *Experiencing God in a Time of Crisis*. London: Meditatio, 2017.

Benefiel, Margaret. *The Soul of a Leader: Finding Your Path to Success and Fulfillment*. New York: Crossroad, 2008.

Benner, David G. *Spirituality and the Awakening Self: The Sacred Journey of Transformation*. Grand Rapids, MI: Brazos Press, 2010.

Bourgeault, Cynthia. *Centering Prayer and Inner Awakening*. Boston: Cowley, 2004.

———. *The Heart of Centering Prayer: Nondual Christianity in Theory and Practice*. Boulder, CO: Shambhala Publications, 2016.

Boykin, Kim. *Zen for Christians: A Beginner's Guide*. San Francisco: Jossey-Bass, 2003.

Burrows, Ruth. *Essence of Prayer*. London: Bloomsbury, 2006.

———. *Guidelines for Mystical Prayer*. Rev. ed. Mahwah, NJ: Paulist Press, 2017.

Casey, Michael. *Sacred Reading: The Ancient Art of Lectio Divina*. Liguori, MO: Liguori. 1995.

Cassian, John. *Conferences*. Translated by Colm Luibheid. The Classics of Western Spirituality. New York: Paulist Press, 1985.

The Cloud of Unknowing (with the Book of Privy Counsel). Translated by Carmen Acevedo Butcher. Boston: Shambala Publications, 2009.

Coakley, Sarah. *God, Sexuality, and the Self: An Essay on "The Trinity."* Cambridge, UK: Cambridge University Press, 2013.

Edwards, Tilden. *Embracing the Call to Spiritual Depth: Gifts for Contemplative Living*. Mahwah, NJ: Paulist Press, 2010.

Farley, Wendy. *The Wounding and Healing of Desire: Weaving Heaven and Earth*. Louisville: Westminster John Knox Press, 2005.

Foster, David. *Contemplative Prayer: A New Framework*. London: Bloomsbury, 2015.

Foster, Richard. *Celebration of Discipline: The Path to Spiritual Growth*. 25th ann. ed. San Francisco: HarperSanFrancisco, 1998.

Freeman, Laurence. *The Selfless Self: Meditation and the Opening of the Heart*. Norwich, UK: Canterbury Press, 2009.

Griffiths, Bede. *The Marriage of East and West*. Springfield, IL: Templegate, 1982.

———. *The New Creation in Christ: Christian Meditation and Community*. Springfield, IL: Templegate Publishers, 1992.

———. *Return to the Center*. Springfield, IL: Templegate Publishers, 1976.

Gutierrez, Gustavo. *We Drink from Our Own Wells: The Spiritual Journey of a People*. Maryknoll, NY: Orbis Books, 2003.

Heuertz, Phileena. *Mindful Silence: The Heart of Christian Contemplation*. Downers Grove, IL: InterVarsity Press, 2018.

———. *Pilgrimage of a Soul: Contemplative Spirituality for the Active Life*. 2nd ed. Downers Grove, IL: InterVarsity Press, 2017.

Holmes, Barbara. *Joy Unspeakable: Contemplative Practices of the Black Church*. 2nd ed. Minneapolis: Fortress Press, 2017.

Keating, Thomas. *The Human Condition: Contemplation and Transformation*. Mahwah, NJ: Paulist Press. 1999.

———. *Open Mind, Open Heart: The Contemplative Dimension of the Gospel*. New York: Continuum, 2002.

Komjathy, Louis. *Introducing Contemplative Studies*. Hoboken, NJ: John Wiley, 2018.

Laird, Martin. *Into the Silent Land: A Guide to the Christian Practice of Contemplation*. New York: Oxford University Press. 2006.

———. *A Sunlit Absence: Silence, Awareness, and Contemplation.* New York: Oxford Press, 2006.

Leclercq, Jean. *The Love of Learning and the Desire for God: A Study of Monastic Culture.* 3rd ed. New York: Fordham University Press, 1982.

Lee, Bo Karen. *Sacrifice and Delight in the Mystical Theologies of Anna Maria van Shurman and Madame Jeanne Guyon.* Notre Dame, IN: University of Notre Dame Press, 2014.

McGinn, Bernard, ed. *The Essential Writings of Christian Mysticism.* New York: Modern Library, 2006.

McIntosh, Mark. *Divine Teaching: An Introduction to Christian Theology.* Malden, MA: Blackwell Publishing, 2008.

Main, John. *Monastery Without Walls: The Spiritual Letters of John Main.* Edited by Laurence Freeman. Norwich, UK: Canterbury Press, 2006.

———. *The Way of Unknowing: Expanding Spiritual Horizons Through Meditation.* Norwich, UK: Canterbury Press, 2011.

———. *Word Into Silence: A Manual for Christian Meditation.* Norwich, UK: Canterbury Press, 2006.

May, Gerald G. *The Awakened Heart: Opening Yourself to the Love You Need.* New York: HarperCollins, 1991.

Merton, Thomas. *The Inner Experience: Notes on Contemplation.* San Francisco: HarperOne, 2003.

Nouwen, Henri. *The Way of the Heart: Desert Spirituality and Contemporary Ministry.* San Francisco: HarperSanFrancisco, 1981.

Panikkar, Raimon. *Christophany: The Fullness of Man.* Translated by Alfred DiLascia. Maryknoll, NY: Orbis Books, 2010.

———. *The Experience of God: Icons of the Mystery.* Minneapolis: Fortress Press, 2006.

Pasquale, Teresa B. *Sacred Wounds: A Path to Healing from Spiritual Trauma.* Atlanta, GA: Chalice Press, 2015.

Quashie, Kevin. *The Sovereignty of Quiet: Beyond Resistance in Black Culture.* New Brunswick, NJ: Rutgers University Press, 2012.

Rohr, Richard. *Everything Belongs: The Gift of Contemplative Prayer.* New York: Crossroad, 2014.

———. *Immortal Diamond: The Search for our True Self.* San Francisco: Jossey-Bass, 2013.

———. *The Naked Now: Learning to See as the Mystics See.* New York: Crossroad, 2009.

Soon-Yeong, Yap, and Chok C. Hiew. *Energy Medicine in CFQ Healing: Healing the Body, Transforming Consciousness.* Self-published, iUniverse, 2002.

Taylor, Charles. *A Secular Age.* Cambridge, MA: Harvard University Press, 2007.

———. *Sources of the Self: The Making of the Modern Identity.* Cambridge, MA: Harvard University Press, 1989.

Taylor-Stinson, Therese. *Ain't Gonna Let Nobody Turn Me Around: Stories of Contemplation and Justice.* New York: Church Publishing, 2017.

Thurman, Howard. *Meditations of the Heart.* Boston: Beacon Press, 1953.

Tiso, Francis V. *Rainbow Body and Resurrection: Spiritual Attainment, the Dissolution of the Material Body, and the Case of Khenpo A Chö.* Berkeley: North Atlantic Books, 2016.

Underhill, Evelyn. *Mysticism: A Study in Nature and Development of Spiritual Consciousness.* Mineola, NY: Dover Publications, 2002. First edition published 1911.

Vasliliev, Vladimir, and Scott Meredith. *Let Every Breath: Secrets of the Russian Breath Masters.* Toronto: Systema Headquarters, 2006.

About the Contributors

Sarah Bachelard is a theologian and priest in Anglican Orders based in Canberra, Australia. She is the founding director of the ecumenical community Benedictus Community Church and has led retreats and taught contemplative prayer nationally and internationally. She is the author of *Experiencing God in a Time of Crisis* and *Resurrection and Moral Imagination*.

BA in classics and history, with honors,
   Australian National University

BA in theology, with honors, Oxford University

PhD in philosophy, Australian National University

Thomas Bushlack, PhD, currently serves as regional director of mission integration with SSM Health in St. Louis, Missouri. Prior to working in health care, he spent ten years in academic teaching and research, focusing on the intersection of contemplative spirituality, virtue ethics, and Catholic social thought. He is also an oblate of St. Benedict through St. John's Abbey in Collegeville, Minnesota; a commissioned presenter of Centering Prayer through Contemplative Outreach, Ltd.; and a trustee of the Trust for the Meditation Process.

BA in theology, St. John's University, Collegeville, Minnesota

MTS, University of Notre Dame, Notre Dame, Indiana

PhD in moral theology, University of Notre Dame,
   Notre Dame, Indiana

Sicco Claus is a high school teacher and the national coordinator of the World Community for Christian Meditation in the Netherlands. He is currently finishing his PhD, focusing on the spirituality of John Main (1926–1982), Benedictine monk and promoter of Christian meditation. Sicco is interested in the ways Main's contemplative approach to life is fruitful within the context of cultural-theoretical explorations and practical fields such as education.

MADiv, University of Tilburg
(formerly Catholic Theological University, Utrecht)

MAPhil, University of Utrecht

PhD researcher, Radboud Univeristy, Nijmegen

Fellow, Titus Brandsma Institute, Nijmegen

Leonardo Corrêa is a Brazilian journalist and the director of communication for the World Community for Christian Meditation. He began practicing Christian meditation in 2008 and is a passionate advocate for the discipline, having lived in community at Meditatio House in London in 2011. He is married to Marciélen and lives in Porto Alegre, South Brazil.

BA in social communication, Pontifical Catholic University of Rio Grande do Sul (PUCRS), Porto Alegre, Brazil

Specialization in philosophy (epistemology), PUCRS, Porto Alegre, Brazil

Phileena Heuertz is an author, spiritual director, yoga instructor, public speaker, and retreat guide with a passion for spirituality and making the world a better place. In 2012, she and her husband, Chris, cofounded Gravity to support the development of consciousness in an effort to respond to the challenging social justice perils of our time. She is the author of *Pilgrimage of the Soul* and *Mindful Silence: The Heart of Christian Contemplation.*

BA in education, Asbury University

MA in Christian spirituality, Creighton University, Omaha, Nebraska

Stuart Higginbotham, an Episcopal priest, is the rector of Grace Episcopal Church, Gainesville, Georgia. His contemplative practice has been nurtured by time with the Shalem Institute for Spiritual Formation and the World Community for Christian Meditation. His current work and writing focuses on the intersection of contemplative practice, leadership development, and congregational ministry. He writes at www.contemplativereformation.com.

BS in biology, Lyon College, Batesville, Arkansas

MDiv, Columbia Theological Seminary, Decatur, Georgia

DMin, The School of Theology at the University of the South, Sewanee, Tennessee

Bo Karen Lee is associate professor of spiritual theology and Christian formation at Princeton Theological Seminary. She received training as a spiritual director from Oasis Ministries and was a Mullin Fellow with the Institute of Advanced Catholic Studies. Her book *Sacrifice and Delight in the Mystical Theologies of Anna Maria van Schurman and Madame Jeanne Guyon* argues that the surrender of self to God can lead to the deepest joy in God. She has recently completed a volume with Margaret Benefiel on *The Soul of Higher Education*, which explores contemplative pedagogies and research strategies. She is also the recipient of the John Templeton Award for Theological Promise.

Yale University, New Haven, Connecticut

MDiv, Trinity International University, Deerfield, Illinois

ThM, Princeton Theological Seminary

PhD, Princeton Theological Seminary

Mark Longhurst is the pastor of First Congregational Church (United Church of Christ) in the Berkshires of Williamstown, Massachusetts. A graduate of the inaugural class of the Living School, with the Center for Action and Contemplation (Albuquerque, NM), he writes and hosts the contemplatively themed blog *Ordinary Mystic* at www.ordinarymystic.net.

BA in English literature and language, Gordon College, Wenham, Massachusetts

MDiv, Harvard Divinity School, Cambridge, Massachusetts

Mark Kutolowski is an oblate of St. Benedict, a contemplative retreat leader, Centering Prayer teacher, and instructor in the traditional Russian martial art and health practice of Systema. He has spent the past twenty years exploring the integration of Christian contemplation with physical transformation, and he teaches on this topic from his family's homestead, Metanoia of Vermont, www.metanoiavt.com.

BA in anthropology, Dartmouth College, Hanover,
New Hampshire

Kirsten Oates has experience in strategic consulting with Bain & Company and the Bridgespan Group as well as a number of nonprofit and faith-based organizations. Kirsten spent eighteen months working with the Center for Action and Contemplation's executive director to develop a future state vision for the organization beyond the life of its founder. As the managing director of programs for the CAC, she is now responsible for ensuring that the CAC's programs are aligned with the Christian contemplative lineage. Kirsten grew up in Australia.

BA in economics, Australian University

BA in laws, with honors, Australian National University

Jessica (Jessie) M. Smith, PhD, is an educator and writer at heart, who is deeply committed to spiritual practice, faith-based civic engagement, and theological reflection. After receiving her doctorate in theological studies from Emory University, she currently serves on the board of directors of the Shalem Institute for Spiritual Formation and on the staff of the General Board of Church and Society of The United Methodist Church in Washington, DC.

BA in English, University of Virginia

MDiv, Candler School of Theology, Emory University

PhD in theological studies, Graduate Division of Religion, Emory University

Matthew Wright is an Episcopal priest, writer, and retreat leader working to renew the Christian wisdom tradition within a wider interspiritual framework. He serves as priest-in-charge at St. Gregory's Episcopal Church in Woodstock, New York, and is a teacher for Northeast Wisdom and The Contemplative Society, nonprofits rooted in the teaching lineage of Cynthia Bourgeault. Matthew lives with his wife, Yanick, alongside the brothers of Holy Cross Monastery in West Park, New York.

BA in religious studies, University of North Carolina, Chapel Hill, North Carolina

MDiv, Virginia Theological Seminary, Alexandria, Virginia

New Contemplative Exchange Founders and Facilitators

 **Tilden Edwards,** Shalem's founder and Senior Fellow, served as Shalem's executive director for over twenty-seven years. An Episcopal priest with parish experience, he is a nationally respected speaker, retreat leader, and author, most recently of *Embracing the Call to Spiritual Depth*. He has designed and led contemplative programs since 1979 and continues to write and teach about the spiritual life.

Laurence Freeman, OSB, is a Benedictine monk of the Monastery of Christ Our Saviour, Turvey, England, a monastery of the Congregation of Mount Oliveto. He is the director of the World Community for Christian Meditation. He is also an internationally renowned speaker, author, and teacher in Christian meditation and interfaith dialogue, including the historic Way of Peace with His Holiness the Dalai Lama. Fr. Laurence has been teaching an MBA course on meditation and leadership at the McDonough School of Business at Georgetown University, Washington, DC, since 2013. In the same year he started to lead a course Health and Meditation: Healing from the Center at the Royal College of Physicians in Ireland.

Thomas Keating, OCSO (1923–2018), was a Cistercian monk and the founder and spiritual guide of Contemplative Outreach, an international organization focused on the development of Centering Prayer. Fr. Thomas was an internationally renowned theologian and author. He traveled the world and spoke with laypeople and communities about contemplative Christian practices and the psychology of the spiritual journey, which is the subject of his *Spiritual Journey* video and DVD series.

Richard Rohr, OFM, is a globally recognized ecumenical teacher bearing witness to the universal awakening within Christian mysticism and the Perennial Tradition. He is a Franciscan priest of the New Mexico Province and founder of the Center for Action and Contemplation in Albuquerque, New Mexico. Fr. Richard is the author of many books, including *Everything Belongs*, *Adam's Return*, *The Naked Now*, *Breathing Under Water*, *Falling Upward*, and *Immortal Diamond*. His latest book is *The Divine Dance: The Trinity and Your Transformation* (with Mike Morrell).

Margaret Benefiel, PhD, is the executive director of the Shalem Institute for Spiritual Formation. Prior to coming to Shalem, she ran Executive Soul, helping leaders and organizations nurture their souls and express their deepest values institutionally. She also taught as adjunct faculty at Andover Newton Theological School in the area of contemplative leadership. Rooted in Quaker practice, Margaret has written extensively on various aspects of contemplative leadership and spirituality at work, including *The Soul of Supervision*; *The Soul of a Leader: Finding Your Path to Fulfillment and Success*; and *Soul at Work: Spiritual Leadership in Organizations*.